Once More With Love

Bobbi Coyle-Hennessey is a nationally recognized leader in divorce recovery work and a trailblazer with her breakthrough program for those considering remarriage after divorce or the death of a spouse. She and her husband, Larry, have conducted their remarriage preparation program for the last ten years. Coyle-Hennessey has also been active in the Beginning Experience and the North American Conference of Separated and Divorced Catholics.

What participants in the *Once More With Love* program say:

"The content is superb, the style very attractive, the program relevant and helpful."

"Thanks for the tools and insights that helped me choose with my head as well as my heart."

"This course is for real, the discussions in-depth, realistic, and open."

"Thanks for the wonderful experience. We learned more about one another in-depth, and we learned to simply take the time to share ourselves with one another."

A Guide to Marrying Again

Once More With Love

Bobbi Coyle-Hennessey

AVE MARIA PRESS   Notre Dame, Indiana 46556

Special Note: The names and experiences used in this book have been altered and generalized in such a way as to protect and respect the privacy of persons. In any instance in which a person might be recognizable, individual permission has been obtained.

"On Marriage" taken from THE PROPHET by Kahlil Gibran. Copyright 1923 by Kahlil Gibran and renewed 1951 by Administrators C.T.A. of Kahlil Gibran Estate and Mary G. Gibran. Reprinted by permission of Alfred A. Knopf, Inc.

The Bible text used in this publication is from the *Good News Bible*: Copyright © American Bible Society 1976. Used with permission. For the United Kingdom, permission granted by the British and Foreign Bible Society and Collins Publishers, London.

This book previously appeared as *Once More With Love: Awareness and Preparation for Remarriage*, published by the author in 1990.

Acknowledgments

*I*n appreciation and gratitude to:

Michelle Hennessey, my sister-in-law and a graphic artist, who designed the cover for the self-published edition of this book and who inspired the design of this edition's cover.

Bob Tomich, whose experiences and prodding moved me to start the *Once More With Love* program and who assisted in facilitating it early on;

Larry Hennessey, my husband and lover, who shares the facilitator spotlight with me;

writer Claire Berman, who wrote the *Reader's Digest* (September 1984) article "What You Should Know Before You Remarry" about our program, and who encouraged me to continue writing with the sage advice, "You need to be a good writer, not necessarily a perfect one";

writers Barbara Zahner, Kathleen Kircher, and Anita Louis who edited my work;

writer Joan O'Hanneson for her expert and professional encouragement in completing this project;

Rev. William O'Keeffe and Rev. Michael J. Rosswurm, who offered suggestions and assistance on religious matters;

writers Don and Barbara Kohles who offered additional professional assistance;

Danette and Jerry Hayes of ExecuStaff for their invaluable advice and assistance in publishing the first printing of this book.

♦

I am deeply grateful to my sons, Michael, Stephen, and David Coyle, my family, my friends, and the separated, divorced, and remarried community who have continued to support and encourage me in this effort.

Once More With Love is dedicated to the many participants of this program whose struggles and successes have shaped this book. It is also dedicated to the memory of Father James J. Young, CSP, founder of The North American Conference of Separated and Divorced Catholics, Inc., who encouraged me to continue the ministry to remarrying couples through this remarriage program.

Contents

Preface

*I*t is finished!

These words echo down through the ten-year struggle to articulate a wonderful program in written form. It has been difficult. I have dotted the last i, completed the last sentence, and closed down the writing of *Once More With Love*.

It is finished, but I know I am also beginning again, because our participants in the *Once More With Love* program continue to nuance our work with their own experience and discovery.

This book was born out of my own painful struggle as a divorced and remarried Catholic looking for support and ministry from the church. I was divorced in the mid-seventies, when the divorce rate was swelling. There were no books, information, or supportive materials available in the secular market, and (to my knowledge) no ministry or support within the Catholic church. Like other divorced Catholics, I felt guilty for not adhering to the teaching of one marriage for life, I felt I was a reject, even though I was working in the church as a religious education teacher and coordinator.

Six months after my husband left, *Creative Divorce* by Mel Kranzler — the first major book dealing with the experience of divorce — hit the bookstores. In reading his book, I learned for the first time that I wasn't crazy. My experiences — the emotional roller coaster ride I was on, and the depression and grief — all were normal. Recovery is slow. It took me two-and-a-half years of pain and stress before I began to feel good again.

During that difficult time, a marvelous opportunity to study for a masters degree in religious education at Seattle University presented itself. I eagerly took up this challenge for three summers, while continuing religious education ministry during the winter months in San Jose. It provided a wonderful chance to grow while recovering from such a painful wound.

In Seattle, I was fortunate to meet Fr. Jim Young, a Paulist priest from Boston who was shepherding a fledgling parish support group ministry through a newly developing national organization, *The North American Conference of Separated and Divorced Catholics (NACSDC)*. I was inspired, through his vision, to develop a support group in the parish in which I was working. I had frequently been called upon by other Catholics for support in their grief following separation and divorce. This was an opportunity to develop awareness in the parish as well as provide a place at church for people to share their pain and find support for their recovery.

I became more deeply involved in NACSDC when I was elected to the Board of Directors as a representative of Western Region 11. As a member of that board for four years, I was introduced to courageous and committed Catholics from other regions of the United States and Canada and to a ministry that was developing rapidly. NACSDC gained strength and support from the separated, divorced, and remarried Catholics who refused to walk away from the church. NACSDC was also gaining respect from the American and Canadian Catholic clergy.

It was my privilege to work with such great visionaries and leaders as the late Fr. Jim Young, the NACSDC chaplain, and Paula Ripple and Kathleen Kircher, the first and second directors of NACSDC respectively. In my travels about the country and my work within the state of California, I was inspired by many Catholic individuals who either worked in this ministry or received the support this ministry provided. NACSDC was on the move, and it was on the cutting edge of separated and divorced ministry. Today, as a result of those many unnamed pioneers and the NACSDC leadership, it is a well-respected organization and is now contributing to the development of ministry to the remarried Catholic.

Four years after my divorce, I met Larry Hennessey, who became my second husband a year later. When I remarried, some doors of church were closed to me that had previously been open, but my relationship with God and my work with NACSDC gave me a sense of belonging and purpose. Following my tenure on the Board of Directors, Larry and I were asked to serve on the Professional Advisory Council to the NACSDC Board representing remarriage concerns. We remained on that council for three years.

As always, when one door closes, another opens. Along with NACSDC ministry, I began a consultant business, *New Beginnings: Divorce Recovery*, in which I offered workshops on divorce recovery. At one of those workshops, a gentleman named Bob, recovering from a second divorce, commented at the end of one session, "I wish I had known about divorce recovery after my first divorce. Maybe if I had, I wouldn't have stepped so quickly into a second marriage unprepared. Have you ever thought of offering a preparation program for people considering remarriage?"

With Bob's inspiration and assistance and Larry's support, I put together a six-week program, which I named *Once More With Love*. The pilot session in 1982 included one newly remarried couple, one engaged couple, two couples going together, and four divorced single persons. The positive evaluations from that pilot group encouraged us and supported our belief that we were on the right track. Bob and I facilitated the program until Larry finished a degree. Eventually, Bob went on to other endeavors, while Larry and I continue to facilitate the program.

Since February 1982, we have offered forty sessions (approximately four a year) and 450 individuals have participated. Six of the participants have repeated the program with a different partner, after the first relationship fell apart.

Our evaluations continue to be positive, which indicates to us that we have a solid program that meets the needs of remarrying couples. Our referrals come from former participants as well as local parishes. The topics we used initially — values, former marital history, problem solving, communication, stepparenting, finances, intimacy and religion — continue to be relevant to our participants. We have made some modifications and appropriate upgrades as needed during these past ten years.

As we have presented our program at conferences and various meetings, many friends throughout the country have asked us for a copy of the materials. My response has been, "I'm writing a book on the program, and I'll let you know when it is finished." I have felt guilty for taking so long, but I work full-time, and don't always feel up to sitting at a computer when I arrive home. Writing is hard work!

And so to all those who have waited so patiently for so long I say to you, "It is finished! Alleluia and amen."

Postscript

I self-published the first edition of *Once More With Love* in

1990. I'm pleased that the book sold throughout the U.S. and in some places in Canada. The *Once More With Love* program is facilitated in several dioceses as well. Today, in 1993, Ave Maria Press has assumed the publishing rights and produced its edition. Life is full of wonderful new beginnings!

Bobbi
1993

Grow old along with me!
the best is yet to be,
the last of life,
for which the first was made.
— Robert Browning
"Rabbi Ben Ezra"

Introduction

Welcome to *Once More With Love*! You are about to embark on a journey of growth and awareness as you examine the challenges of remarriage.

Why are you reading this book? In our experience with other groups, we have discovered several reasons for people attending our *Once More With Love* classes:

- ◆ Some participate as part of their parish's or church's preparation for their second marriage.

- ◆ Others, not previously married, are engaged to a previously married person and want to prepare for the future.

- ◆ Some want to clarify issues in order to decide responsibly whether or not to marry.

- ◆ Already married couples seek support and answers to tough, unexpected situations.

- ◆ Singles want to explore remarriage so that they will be better equipped to choose a mate, to commit to a lifelong loving relationship, and to avoid marital failure.

Current statistics indicate that for every two new marriages entered into each year, an existing marriage breaks up. Approximately 75 percent of divorced persons remarry, and the divorce rate for second and subsequent marriages is expected to be about 10 percent higher than for first marriages. The most frequent break-ups occur to those who remarry within two years of the first divorce. These statistics startle us because one would think that we learn from our past mistakes; therefore, divorces should not occur so readily the second time.

Many factors contribute to the failure of second marriages, and there are some useful strategies for coping with the issues and problems that arise. Through *Once More With Love*, we hope to increase your awareness of these factors and strategies as we invite you and your partner to review your past history, your present relationship, and your future goals as individuals and as a couple.

15

We never expect couples who go through the program to marry as a result. We want to assist you in developing communication and conflict resolution skills so that you can more responsibly choose the direction of your relationship and manage potential problems. If you decide you need more time before marital commitment or that you really are not suited to each other and choose to end the relationship, the process has been as much of a success for you as for those who conclude that they are indeed on the right track and wish to continue toward a permanent, loving, married commitment.

We want to support you in your journey and suggest ways and resources that will deepen and enrich your relationship. We will share some of our own story and insights regarding remarriage, as well as stories and insights drawn from the many couples we've worked with over the years. Although the *Once More With Love* program is designed with Catholic couples in mind, most of the concerns we address are universal to any couple considering remarriage or already in a second marriage.

As you work through the chapters, whether on your own or with a group, we encourage you to reflect on and share your own story, insights, and concerns. The worksheets at the end of each chapter will give you the opportunity to clarify your thoughts and open discussion on the many issues involved in remarriage.

Let us begin!

CHAPTER 1

Preparation, Feelings, and Values

*E*verything that happens in this world happens at the
time God chooses.
[God] sets the time for birth and the time for death,
the time for planting and the time for pulling up,
the time for killing and the time for healing,
the time for tearing down and the time for building.
[God] sets the time for sorrow and the time for joy,
the time for mourning and the time for dancing.

— *Ecclesiastes 3:1–4*

Preparation

When we prepare for a second marriage, we need to review the
two major factors that contribute to the failure of second marriages:
1) marrying too soon after divorce; 2) marrying without awareness
of potential second marriage problems. Many people enter a second
marriage before they are emotionally and psychologically ready to
form a new, healthy, lifelong commitment. Although the divorce
proceedings from the first marriage are completed, persistent attachment to the former spouse continues and may impede the loving
commitment needed in a new marital relationship. Frequently, the
provoked aggravation, harassment, and revenge tactics that some
former spouses direct toward each other during and after divorce
signify residual, deep-seated attachment.

Robert Weiss in his book *Marital Separation* states:

Attachment seems, at least in many individuals, to have an
imprinted quality; once a certain other has been accepted

17

as an attachment figure, that person can again elicit attachment feelings, at least until he or she is understood as
having become intrinsically different.[1]

When separation and divorce occur, the accompanying loneliness motivates many to search desperately for a new nurturing,
understanding partner to fill that empty space left by the former
spouse and to provide much-needed happiness and self-esteem. In
effect, recently divorced person who enter into hasty new relationships reassure themselves and proclaim to the world, "See, I'm
OK — someone loves and needs me." Sadly, this intense desire to
recouple often drives the newly divorced into unsuccessful second
marriages.

Divorce Recovery

Divorce, a painful crisis and a major life change, demands
ample time for recovery and for acceptance of the ongoing residual
effects of the first marriage and divorce. Some psychologists esti-
mate that a minimum transitional time of two years is required.
Others stretch it to five or more years, suggesting it takes one year
of recovery for every five years of marriage. The following timetable
illustrates a typical recovery process of an individual.

Year	Issues and Dynamics
1st year	Grieves over loss; survives minute-to-minute; experiences emotional, psychological, economical, spiritual instability; lacks self-esteem and confidence; sometimes feels suicidal; focuses primarily on the past.
2nd year	Lets go of past; begins to heal, cope, start anew; develops single identity, forms new social ties and support; reorganizes goals, work, economic status; focuses more on the future.
3rd year	Feels positive, stable, confident, worthwhile most of the time; re-establishes control of one's life; thrives; acknowledges some personal responsibility for the marital failure.

4th year   Integrates divorce crisis into overall life experience; recognizes personal growth inherent in divorce experience; stabilizes personal adult autonomy.

Although this timetable is general, it matches the experience of many individuals, especially those who have been left rather than those who leave the marriage. Usually those who leave initially experience relief or peacefulness, for they have grieved the loss of marital happiness while still in the marriage, sometimes even before divorce is considered. However, these "leavers" also experience additional feelings of loss and instability after leaving.

Each individual recovers in his or her own time. Some get stuck in denial, anger, bitterness, or attachment, thus blocking recovery. Others may grieve longer due to emotional problems or blocks. They may need therapy to learn how to cope during the recovery period. Partners in briefer marriages — five years or less — may sustain fewer residual emotional effects than those in longer marriages. Social scientists and psychologists are still evaluating the divorce process and its long-term effects on all family members.

I remember the lingering sadness I felt from an unexpected source of grief. It didn't show up until ten years after my divorce and five years into a happy second marriage. About eight years ago, my husband Larry and I attended two silver anniversary parties of first-married friends and one golden anniversary celebration, all within a five-month period. Surprised by my deep feelings of unrest and pain at those events — feelings I couldn't account for — I began to journal about them. As I did so, I began to understand that my jealousy, anger, and depression were rooted in grief over the loss of the one perfect lifetime marriage and intact family. I grieved the loss of the fantasy of living "happily ever after."

When I have shared this experience with others, many have substantiated it by sharing similar feelings. Others have an "aha" experience as they are finally able to name an unexpressed grief of their own.

Those anniversary celebrations highlighted for me the joy that families experience in growing through marriage and family development. The staying power and rewards of a lifelong marital history — the birth and raising of children, surviving the teenage years, the empty nest and change of life, family traditions and joyful family gatherings, the triumph over economic crises and psychological rewards of a lifetime marriage — are beautiful and nostalgic for me. I felt deep sadness at the loss of that dream, of the expectation that was a part of the "I do's" of my first marriage. Once I identified those feelings and acknowledged them, I found that the grief greatly subsided. That particular wound has healed.

Do not misconstrue my comments. My marriage to Larry is wonderful — but different. We are not raising children. We are in mid-life stages. We have created a wonderful thirteen-year history together full of our own crises and rewards that enrich our relationship. As each of our anniversaries comes to pass, we celebrate our life, our history, our love. The older I get, the more I value my children, my family, and my life experience, including both of my marriages. I look forward to a rich celebration of twenty-five years with Larry.

Recovery is stressful work. It demands self-evaluation, coping with feelings of failure, guilt, anger, rejection, fear, loneliness, and readjusting life dreams and expectations. One must let go of the past marriage relationship, learn to accept and forgive the former spouse and oneself, and create a new life. Reverend James J. Young, CSP, deceased past chaplain to the *North American Conference of Separated and Divorced Catholics (NACSDC)*,[2] names this achievement of re-integration "adult autonomy." Sometimes therapy provides the time, distance, and objectivity to assist in the recovery process and the journey to adult autonomy. Perhaps my personal story will highlight this painful but growth-filled journey.

For twenty years I was a happily married woman with a great husband, three fine sons and a busy suburban life. Eighteen years ago I was thrust, kicking and screaming, into the single world of the divorced, totally unprepared for the changes that awaited me. In my thirty-eight years, I had never lived alone or even had my own bedroom. I depended on my lifestyle — husband, children, house with a white picket fence, volunteer work, suburban socials — for my happiness and self-esteem. Seeing this lifestyle in ashes, I felt afraid, rejected, angry, guilt-ridden, and unbearably lonely. I felt unstable and suicidal. I could not believe that I would survive this crisis, or ever feel happiness again.

Yet, with the assistance and loving support of my family and some special friends and the persistent desire to survive, I journaled my way through the pain, anger, and depression. I prayed and struggled with my identity. I tapped into God's grace within — the power that nudged me to begin again. I challenged my fears into steppingstones: I went back to school; I took up the banjo; I changed jobs; I bought my first car; I traveled whenever finances permitted; I started a support group and a part-time business. Soon, the fresh green shoots of new life poked through my winter darkness and I celebrated small accomplishments with gigantic "alleluias!" Within three years my enthusiasm for life returned.

As I journeyed from death to resurrection, I relied on God's absolute, unconditional love of me and discovered my God-given uniqueness and giftedness. I developed a variety of caring friendships, a creative career, and a ministry of outreach. I discovered that happiness originates from within me rather than from others. I unwrapped my most painful wound of divorce and discovered the wonderful gift of a new me!

Unfortunately, some divorced persons view the single life as a waiting station between marriages. They remarry during those painful transitional stages of recovery, choosing someone whose presence fills the sudden lonely spaces or nurturing or dependency needs. Later, they often discover that their new "transitional" partner does not meet their long-term needs for mutual love, compatibility, and permanence.

Sometimes the remarrying person brings to the new relationship so much unfinished business from the past failed marriage that the new marriage flounders. When a second divorce occurs, its chaos arouses all the unfinished grieving of the past. For example, Albert, an engineer from New Jersey, tells of leaving his first twenty-year marriage, changing jobs, moving to California, meeting and marrying another woman with children, all within six months.

Al states:

> I suspected within a month of the marriage that it was a mistake but I decided to remain in the marriage. Three years, thousands of dollars, and a bitter court battle later, we were divorced. I spent more time and money divorcing my second wife than living with her in marriage.

Al emerged from this "marry-go-round" feeling inadequate and angry because of the emotional and financial devastation of the two recent divorces. He also acknowledged how unprepared he was for the problems inherent in a second union.

Another confused and depressed woman sat nervously wringing her hands as she explained to me the two litigations she was involved in: one, a custody battle over the children from the first marriage; the second, court proceedings over the property settlement from the second union. She had remarried a year after her first divorce.

These are not isolated incidents. Their frequency substantiates the need for divorced people to recover sufficiently from the marital break-down before entering another serious relationship. When someone has heart surgery, doctors will advise the recovering patient to limit physical stress and gradually increase physical exercise in order to heal properly and recover the strength to live a normal life. If the patient disregards the advice, rushing into activity too soon, he may end up back in the hospital or even dead. Similarly, the seeds of failure of a remarriage can often be found in the inadequate time taken for emotional and psychological recovery and healing from the first marital break-up.

Today, an alternative to remarriage exists. Some individuals choose to remain single following divorce because of the growing awareness and acceptance of the single life as a viable, pleasing lifestyle. They live fulfilled, happy, and successful lives as single persons. Others acknowledge that perhaps they should never have married in the first place because their lifestyle may not be compatible with married life, or they are no longer willing to make the inevitable accommodations necessary for a committed lifelong love relationship. Consequently, they choose not to remarry.

When I first met thirty-eight-year-old Susan, experiencing a traumatic divorce after sixteen years of marriage, she felt worthless, rejected, and guilty, and she was toying with suicide. She doubted she would survive the emotional and economic crisis. She persevered, however, and during the next two years she picked up the pieces of her life, joined a support group, updated her nursing skills, and subsequently found employment at a local hospital. Two and a half years later, I encountered a new Susan — a friendly, self-assured woman who exuded real joy. She said to me:

> I do not need marriage to be happy. I have survived on my own and I'll never compromise who I am for anyone ever

again! I really feel wonderful for the first time ever. I am far more selective about the men I date. Even though I really want to be married again, I don't want to marry just to avoid loneliness. I want to share my life with someone who shares similar values with me and affirms me as an equal partner in the relationship. Sometime I hope to meet him. However, until I do, I prefer to be a happy single than an unhappy married.

Susan, like many divorced women who take the time to recover, no longer looks for a Prince Charming or wants to be a Princess on a Pedestal. She knows herself well and knows the kind of marriage she wants and the kind of person with whom she will choose to spend her life. She wants to avoid past mistakes and, at the same time, recognizes that there are no guarantees to the fairy tale of living happily ever after.

Remarriage Concerns

Besides jumping in too soon, second marriages frequently fail because the partners do not consider the complex issues inherent in a second union. These factors include values, problem solving, stepparenting, finances, previous marital history, and religion. Generally, we enter first marriages in our young adult years or the early twenties. We are still psychologically separating from our parents as well as defining our values as we develop our own lifestyle. During this maturing time, we explore and challenge our values, our wants, and our needs. We pursue career goals, economic and social status, friendships, marriage, and parenting.

As we mature, we develop a stronger self-identity and value-identity and want to be true to our beliefs. We tend to be more open, honest, and direct in our relationships with others. We become less flexible about what we will and will not accept in our lives. If a divorce occurs during these maturing years, the foundation of our whole life crumbles and we begin to analyze and evaluate our most cherished beliefs. This self-analysis accelerates our personal growth.

We bring into a second union an accumulated adult history, which not only includes the previous marriage and divorce, but also children and custody agreements. Former in-laws, friends, family traditions, and established lifetime habits are part of the package. Most likely one or both of the partners built some financial status — investments, a home, inheritances, and multiple incomes. Our responsibilities may include extensive debts, spousal and child support, and partial support of aging parents. We also grapple with unfinished religious issues such as annulments, membership, participation, or alienation from church, reconciliation and forgiveness. If partners lack the awareness and preparation to handle these stressful, complex issues, second marriages frequently fail.

Feelings

We begin with feelings and values because so much of our behaviors and our choices and decisions in life are derived consciously and unconsciously from the beliefs and standards we carry within us. When we disclose values, we need to speak about our feelings, not just our thoughts. In revealing our hidden hopes, fears, insecurities, dreams, and expectations, we open communication with our inner selves. We cannot expect our partner to read our mind or to understand some of our expectations unless we speak of them and of the emotions that surround them.

Feelings emerge spontaneously from deep within us. Since we don't "plan" our feelings, we cannot judge them harshly. Feelings just are. Once we acknowledge and accept them, we usually can control how we express or act on them. For example, I may feel angry at my partner for being late for an important meeting. That feeling in itself is not bad. If, however, I deny the anger, become accusatory and attacking to hurt my partner, or if I retreat in an angry pout, these actions can be judged negatively, since I am using my anger in a retaliatory way. As the anger intensifies, stress builds. If I continue this behavior, I will build a wall between us or explode in an inappropriate way. On the other hand, I can build a bridge of communication and closeness by risking the disclosure of my feelings and working with my partner to resolve the conflict. We need to direct our spontaneous feelings outward in an appropriate way so that they do not encumber us or inappropriately hurt others.

Ken and Becky Eggeman, educators and trainers of *Marriage and Family Development* in Southern Hills, Indiana, give three steps necessary to maintain and preserve emotional growth and stability in ourselves and in our marriages:

Step 1: We need to recognize that we have emotions and will always have emotions. By this recognition, we are also saying that our mate has emotions and will always have emotions.

Step 2: We need to accept our feelings. Feelings ARE, and they are OK. "I am angry, and that is OK. My mate is angry, and that is OK."

Step 3: We need to share our feelings and act appropriately. We need to speak from our "self" and use "I" in our sharing. In so doing, we will avoid the pitfalls of trouble, like blaming, attacking, taking flight, rationalizing, using we/they. Therefore, we assume responsibility for our feelings.[3]

Values

When we speak of our feelings, we may ask ourselves, "Why do I feel this way?" or "Where does that feeling come from?" With self-examination, we can discover how our emotions connect to our basic value system. Values begin at birth as we absorb information and behavior standards through observation of our parents and extended families, our first nurturers and role models. Further development occurs through association with our peers, schools, churches, media, culture, and society. In our teens, we begin to model and challenge some of those values. By the time we reach our twenties, our core values and attitudes are stabilized into our behavior, although we may not be able to identify many of them. Thereafter, it usually takes a significant emotional event or crisis to jolt and challenge us into re-evaluating or changing our values. Divorce is one of those major life-events.

I propose that our value system can be divided into three levels, although there are no definite lines of demarcation. The central or core system is most deeply imbedded and significant to our behavior. A second or intermediate level, less intense, is more flexible and probably more conscious. We also hold peripheral values, which are easily changed according to the times and status of our lives.

For example, a core value might be the spirituality of a person, based on an early and strong religious upbringing. It may be expressed by a strong desire to be a part of a specific religious community, such as the Catholic church, and is patterned through active participation in the parish. This person may expect a marriage partner to make regular participation in church a high priority. Another core value could be the expectation that the family follow the traditional roles of husband as head of the household and wife as caretaker of the home and children. A career-minded wife or family-oriented husband may be unacceptable as a marriage partner in such a case.

An intermediate value may be an individual's need for orderliness and organization. Such a person may be willing to be flexible or make exceptions — though a bit uncomfortably — as appears appropriate to a particular situation. For instance, Mary and Jim have planned a heavy weekend of necessary yard work. On Sunday, Jim, prompted by the warm sunny day, spontaneously suggests a barbecue at the park to complete the day. Even though Mary hesitates, as unfinished gardening nags at her, she remembers that it has been awhile since she and Jim have relaxed together.

A peripheral value could be the hobbies one chooses or the clothing style one wears. These may vary and change from time to time. In college days, a person may prefer football or contact sports for recreation. Later, that same person may value a quieter activity such as golf or sailing.

A core value for one person can be a peripheral value for another; moreover, values can conflict. A conflict in core values between marital partners will very likely strain the relationship, while similar or compatible core values between partners enhance a relationship. A couple may marry, then discover that one has a strong "workaholic" attitude toward the job while the other believes family comes first. These two core values and the expectations that surround them will frequently clash. Unless there is some effort to resolve this conflict creatively and accommodate the other's value system, the couple will probably not enjoy a harmonious relationship, and may end up in the divorce court.

A value system may be open or closed. Openness allows for another perspective even though it may not be a personal choice. A closed view holds that one's personal view is the only acceptable and correct one. "I am right and you are wrong" generates real battles! In remarriage, an open value system appears essential given the previous adult history and the issues the couple will have to face. We need to acknowledge and affirm that each of us views life uniquely based upon our own personality, upbringing, and life experience, and that our individual perspectives are not necessarily wrong, just different. When we are acquainted with and accepting of one another's perspective, our relationships are enriched and more peaceful.

When Larry and I were first married we noticed some differences in the way we fold laundry. He folds towels sides toward the middle; I fold sides together. We discussed, rather heatedly, which was "correct," then began laughing at the absurdity of the quarrel. Rather than argue which was right, we shared what we were taught at home. Today each of us still folds laundry according to our own "tradition," but without criticism from the other. We are just glad that the towels get folded!

Some of our couples have noticed that their arguments erupt over semantics, the differences in the understood meaning of the words they use, rather than real differences in their values or preferences. Frequently, word meanings are loaded with emotional and personal family history connotations. John and Mary Smith's quarrel over "leftovers" illustrates the divisive effect of semantics.

Mary began: "To prepare for Sunday dinner guests, I began a rice dish one Saturday afternoon which required twelve cups of pre-cooked rice. John accused me of planning to serve 'leftovers' to our guests."

John added: "We got into quite an argument over the meaning of the word 'leftovers.' In my family, mom prepares a meal on the day of its serving so it is fresh. Anything that spends the night in the refrigerator and is served the next day is considered leftovers. So when Mary fixed the rice on Saturday, I determined it to be a 'leftover' on Sunday."

Mary countered: "In my family, my mom prepares as much of the meal as possible in advance so that she can spend more time with her guests. Leftovers are anything from the meal that remains uneaten."

"Once we cooled down," concluded John, with a chuckle, "we talked about our individual perceptions of 'leftovers.' We understand each other better now and we no longer quarrel over 'leftovers.'"

Values can reflect cultural differences as well. For example, in the United States we hold our eating utensils differently than Europeans. We move our forks from right to left to right hand as we cut and eat our food. Europeans keep their forks in the same hand for both cutting and eating. Neither approach is right or wrong, just different. It helps to become aware of differences in ourselves and others while maintaining our own values and preferences.

I was once invited to an Italian Christmas Day dinner. The meal began with antipasto, salad, spaghetti and meatballs, french bread, and sliced ham. The hostess then served the turkey, mashed and sweet potatoes, gravy, and vegetables, followed by several traditional desserts, plus the pumpkin and apple pies, and a variety of beverages. I was overwhelmed by the unexpected amount of food; nevertheless, it was the traditional Christmas dinner of that family, and it spoke clearly of the intermingling of their Italian and American values and culture.

Finally, real values are determined by whether we live by them or just talk about them. Dr. Maury Smith, in his book A *Practical Guide to Values Clarification*, suggests the following checklist for determining our values:

♦ A value must be chosen freely.

♦ A value must be chosen from alternatives.

♦ A value must be chosen after considering the consequences.

♦ A value must be performed.

♦ A value becomes a pattern of life.

♦ A value is cherished.

♦ A value is publicly affirmed.

♦ A value enhances the person's total growth.[4]

When we measure our values against this criteria, we can determine our true values. To say that I highly value being on time for appointments when I am regularly late is only giving lip service to the value. If I believe church is important in my life, I will participate regularly and practice the tenets of my faith. One divorced friend in his late forties does not wish to raise any more children, so he avoids dating people who are still raising young children. Larry cannot tolerate smoking, and when single, he refused to seriously date anyone who smoked.

Frequent value-conflict occurs because we don't live in an isolated world. Sometimes priorities must be set as to what a particular situation requires. I uphold the speed laws because I believe in their validity. Yet, to save someone's life, I may break the law. I may love another person very much but discover that we are in conflict over religious issues. This may be such a stumbling block in our relationship that I may choose to terminate the relationship. Perhaps my partner has a violent temper or uses alcohol excessively. Although we are compatible in many ways, and we care for each other, I fear the destructiveness of the behavior and decide to end the relationship. My partner and I may disagree on how to prepare a meal, how to furnish our home, or what type of vacation we prefer. Because we love each other and wish to preserve the integrity of our marriage, we may adjust our expectations of each other and work to accommodate each other's needs and values.

A helpful tool in learning more about yourself and your partner is found in the book *Please Understand Me* by David Keirsey and Marilyn Bates.[5] It includes a short quiz, similar to the Myers-Briggs Indicator, that each of you can take to determine which of the sixteen basic personality temperaments you have. It also provides descriptions of the various types.

The more you understand about yourself and your loved one, the more accommodating and accepting you can be of each other. For example, two personality types that the book describes are *introvert* and *extrovert*. An introvert is energized from within and needs to organize and think things through before expressing an opinion. An extrovert is energized from external experiences and by people. Extroverts organize and express opinions quite easily, incorporating responses from others to further clarify their own opinions, sometimes even reversing them!

In our marriage, Larry is the introvert and I am the extrovert. When we go to movies or attend an event, I usually buzz with opinions and ideas, and with lots of energy. Before I understood the difference between us in this particular area, I would get upset and frustrated with Larry when he didn't have an opinion immediately. When I asked, "What do you think?" he would say, "I don't know." Now that I understand how he processes information, I don't have to make him wrong. I just wait patiently until he has organized his thoughts. Meanwhile, I can ask others for immediate feedback if I need it. When he does express his thoughts, they are wonderful gems and well worth waiting for!

Another system of self-evaluation and personal growth called the enneagram can also be useful for couples who want to know themselves and the other better. The word enneagram comes from the Greek: *ennea* (nine) and *gramma* (points). Its ancient symbol of nine points is one of transformation and change. The enneagram of one's personality combines psychology and spirituality for the purpose of self-understanding and self-acceptance. Each person can identify himself or herself in terms of one of the nine numbers.

The insights gathered from undertaking this study provide us with ways to examine the motivation behind our behavior — why we do the things we do. It helps us recognize our gifts and the traps that can turn these gifts into compulsions. This system provides another way in which we can understand ourselves and others. I have found it useful for understanding myself and my family.

A number of books have been published in recent years on this system. *The Enneagram — A Journey of Self-Discovery*[6] by Maria Beesing, O.P., Robert J. Nogosek, C.S.C., and Patrick H. O'Leary, S.J. is a good first book to read and discover which of the nine points best describes you. Another book, *Discovering the Enneagram — An Ancient Tool for a New Spiritual Journey,*[7] by Richard Rohr and Andreas Ebert, is a wise second choice for further personal reflection and development. The more we know about ourselves the better we can relate to others.

Conclusion

During the next few weeks, you will be discussing your values and preferences with each other using the worksheets at the end of each chapter. The topics include your past marital history, conflict, stepparenting, finances, intimacy, and religion. The statements and questions will assist you in surfacing some of your own preferences, values, and feelings, as well as potential conflict areas to explore so that you may better understand and appreciate each other. Some of the statements may appear redundant or may not apply to you. Take the time, however, to review each one for the personal enrichment the discussion may offer each of you. In your responses, be honest; share your feelings and the life history that supports your values. When you do, you help your partner know, understand, and feel close to you.

In the 1970s, the Stanford Research Institute researched how we communicate our feelings. Their findings indicated that 7 percent of our feelings are expressed by the words we use, 35 percent by our body language, and 68 percent by our tone of voice. When you are listening to your loved one, tune in to more than just the words. Listen with your heart to the feelings expressed in the tone of voice. Pay attention to the body language. These efforts will enable you to hear the full message your partner is sharing.

Avoid criticism and judgment of your partner's feelings or preferences. Remember they are neither right nor wrong, they just are. Look for the enrichment that your unique perspectives bring to your relationship. If conflict emerges, note the areas in the margin for reference, further discussion, or possible problem solving at another time.

I hope you will use this communication time as special quality time — a gift of love you give to each other. Let nothing interfere with the time except emergencies. You may want to spread it over two or three sessions during the week so that it doesn't become burdensome. This allows each of you to have time for personal reflection on the insights you are gaining about yourselves and each other.

Values
WORKSHEET

Privately answer the questions, or respond to the statements with *Agree* or *Disagree*. Then share with your partner. Be specific. Include your feelings and how you arrived at that position.

1. What do I look for in a relationship/marriage?

2. What are my "wants"; my "must haves"?

3. What are my "unacceptables"?

4. How do I feel about remaining single the rest of my life?

5. What are my fears about marrying again?

6. My weaknesses and my strengths are . . .

7. Do I wish to change or am I satisfied as I am?

8. My partner's weaknesses and strengths are . . .

9. Does he/she wish to change or is he/she satisfied?

10. Am I willing to accept and live with his/her weaknesses or human limitations for the rest of my life?

11. How do I know that what I want in my new relationship is really present and what I don't want is absent?

12. What would cause me to want a divorce from another marriage?

13. Am I willing to give up things or provide things to accommodate my partner's needs?

14. Am I able to be open, sharing my deepest feelings, anxieties or fears, or do I hold back?

15. Am I trustworthy, honest? Is my partner? How do I know?

16. Do we enjoy many of the same things, share some of the same goals? Name some personal goals for this marriage.

17. Am I basically a happy person with or without a partner, or do I need others to make me happy?

18. Has our courtship been relatively smooth and enjoyable, or do we often have conflict and arguments?

19. Is there a feeling of enduring friendship between us?

20. Am I willing to accept responsibility as far as that is reasonable for making this relationship work?

21. Am I committed to this relationship regardless of the problems?

22. Do I have any doubts that I have made the right choice of a partner?

23. My partner is a good companion to have when doing things together.

24. I am often bothered by the cutting remarks my partner makes about me.

25. I sometimes worry about my partner's temper.

26. My partner has certain mannerisms or habits which annoy me.

27. My partner's moodiness bothers me.

28. My partner is possessive of me.

29. List some expectations you have of your partner in marriage.

30. I am content with what my partner expects of me in marriage.

31. I have some objections to our relationship/marriage.

32. I find that I am at ease with my partner most of the time.

33. Sometimes I am unable to express my true feelings adequately to my partner.

34. Most of the time I can count on my partner to be a good, non-judgmental listener.

35. Often I am displeased with my partner's appearance.

36. I can count on my partner's support when I feel let down.

37. There is no possible way we can have problems in our marriage.

38. Most of the time I am satisfied with life.

39. I am a morning/night person. (mark one)

40. My partner is a morning/night person. (mark one)

41. My partner and I laugh together easily.

42. I am ready for this relationship/marriage.

43. Neither of us feels we are being pushed into marriage.

Additional Comments:

Human Characteristics

How many of these characteristics do you look for in a life partner? How many do you exhibit in yourself? Choose and prioritize in the order of importance the ten most important qualities. Feel free to add some of your own.

	Partner	Self	Priority
1. religious			
2. sense of humor			
3. physically attractive			
4. organized			
5. intellectual			
6. generous toward self and others			
7. extroverted			
8. high self-esteem			
9. confident			
10. high degree of honesty			
11. physically and verbally affectionate			
12. sensitive to others' feelings			

	Partner	Self	Priority
13. neatness in appearance and living habits			
14. introverted			
15. prefers TV entertainment			
16. quiet			
17. spontaneous and enthusiastic			
18. flexible and adaptable			
19. socially oriented			
20. musical			
21. enjoys the arts			
22. sports minded			
23. risk taker			
24. introspective			
25. loves and wants children			
26. friendly			
27. takes responsibility for own actions			
28. macho			
29. sensitive			
30. committed to monogamous marriage			
31. loves to travel			
32. non-abuser of drugs/alcohol			
33. cheerful and positive outlook			
34. feminine			
35. prefers quiet evenings at home			
36. loving and nurturing			
37. willing to share household responsibilities			
38. high level of moral standards			
39. punctual			
40. willing to work together on projects			
41. expresses personal feelings easily			
42. creative and clever			
43. high interest in work or profession			
44. competitive			
45. trustworthy			
46. physically active			

Love is an emotion
So complete that it encompasses
your entire being
You feel like
you are a part
of the other person
Love is an excitement
a sharing
a truth
a unity
Love makes your body more alive
your soul more tender
and your life more beautiful
Because of you
I am able to feel
the true meaning of love

Susan Polis Schutz

CHAPTER 2

Forgiveness, Previous Marital History, Creative Problem Solving

Then Peter came to Jesus and asked, "Lord, if my brother keeps sinning against me, how many times do I have to forgive him? Seven times?"

"No, not seven times," answered Jesus, "but seventy times seven..."

— *Matthew 18:21–22*

Bonnie hesitated, opened the family album for the first time in months. The photographs of their growing children, family vacations, Christmases and birthdays triggered a flood of painful memories as she gazed at the faces of a lifetime ago. The sadness at the failure of that first marriage overwhelmed her and a few tears spilled from her eyes. She closed the book with a sigh, remembering...remembering.

The phone's abrupt ring brought her back into the present. "Hello?...Oh, John, it's you. ... Sure I can hold dinner a while longer. Don't forget our meeting tonight. Thanks, honey, for calling. ... Love you, bye."

We cannot forget or disregard the past. We are shaped by our life experiences and the significant people in our lives. Music, pictures, holiday traditions and gatherings, and conversations trigger bittersweet or angry memories of our past marriage. We sometimes suppress them, but the memories return repeatedly until we confront them, or until we acknowledge and accept them as past memories, understand the trigger mechanism, and then let them go.

When our feelings surrounding these occasions confuse us, we can share them with a caring, listening friend or counselor in order to put them back in perspective. Expressing our emotions helps clear our psychological life of excess blockage, allowing openness to a new beginning which may include a new marriage.

When we bond with someone as intimately as we do in marriage, we invest love, trust, our very selves, and our future well-being in that person. When it ends, we feel disillusionment, unbelievable loss, betrayal, guilt, and anger.

Some partners gradually grow apart, from neglect of their relationship, or from major differences in value systems. Sometimes marriages end because of the couple's inability to cope with outside pressures such as mental or physical disability or severe illness. Financial difficulties or work obsessions frequently strain relationships. Physical or chemical abuses also contribute to marital failure.

Regardless of the reasons for marital breakdown, we must accept our own culpability and forgive ourselves and our partner, recognizing that we all experience human limitation and sinfulness (the capability of deliberately hurting someone, or breaking a religious or moral law). Furthermore, we must be willing to make amends whenever possible and carry out any responsibilities toward our former partner and children of that union such as shared custody, and spousal and/or child support. These legal obligations bind the responsible Christian as moral obligations; one should not contemplate a second marriage unless these essential obligations are in process or completed.

To succeed in a second marriage, we must fully grieve and recover from the first marital failure. Any unfinished business such as bitterness, guilt, incomplete legalities, or a romanticized view of the past partner or marriage interferes and stresses the new relationship at a time when all our energies are needed to build a close, abiding love. These negative feelings mar our own well-being and seriously inhibit chances for happiness in a second union. Divorce recovery, acceptance, forgiveness, and fulfillment of the consequential responsibilities complete closure on the previous marriage and leave us open to a fresh start.

Forgiveness

Forgiveness, an affair of the heart, is possible only with God. When we have been deeply hurt, our natural instincts move us toward punishment, retaliation, or revenge. With God we can begin to let go of those natural responses and work toward forgiveness of the other and the action.

It is helpful to know that forgiveness does not imply approval of the behavior that offends us nor does the matter have to end in reconciliation. Many times neither is possible, yet forgiveness can occur within us with God's help. Sometimes the hurt has been so great that the most we can do is pray for the desire to forgive. That is the first step and may be the only step one can manage in the face of severe hurt. God understands that and even praying for that desire will help us forgive.

The task of forgiveness occurs in small steps with time, distance, objectivity, and prayer. Commenting on forgiveness, Jim Greteman, CSC, in his book *Coping With Divorce* writes, "Forgiveness is a choice, not a feeling. You can decide to forgive, even if your feelings say — not yet. At some point you have to decide to forgive."[1] Forgiveness is not condescending, self-righteous, or conditional. It is given freely and the wrong is forgotten (although the incident itself may not be forgotten). When forgiveness cannot be communicated to the other, it can still be given in the heart through prayer.

I remember the intense anger I felt when my marriage fell apart. Torn between seething revenge and a fledgling desire to forgive, I prayed, "God, please love and forgive him because I can't right now." That was the best effort I could muster at the time, but it was an important step for me. I believed God would do what I could not. Eventually I gained the grace and strength to forgive and accept myself, my former spouse, and the divorce. In letting go of that destructive anger, I created a place for healing to take root, and opened my life to new possibilities. I will never forget those difficult times; however, I no longer harbor bitterness about them. I cherish my resulting growth instead.

Sometimes one partner of the former marriage harasses the other partner or a new marriage through the children, even though two separate lives are established and privacy should be respected by both parties. The retaliatory and vengeful feelings that surface burden us, sap our energy, destroy our inner peace, and jeopardize our present relationships. When we cannot peacefully co-exist, reasonable communication methods need to be developed, such as minimum contact by phone or mail, so that necessary co-parenting or business with a former spouse does not escalate into major war.

At the very least, as former partners, we should agree to maintain a respectful truce when in the company of our children.

One of our class participants told me of an incident of real pain for a friend, Linda, who lived with her for a year while she finished college and prepared to wed her fiance.

> Linda's parents had bitterly divorced while Linda was in high school. Each had remarried and lived in separate parts of the country. Both parents came to the wedding but, because of their unresolved anger from the unhappy divorce years before, they were unable to put aside the rancor, even for their daughter's wedding. At the groom's dinner, they argued over past hurts, causing guests to become uncomfortable and Linda to leave the party in tears. On the wedding day, the battle of snide remarks and put-downs continued, as each parent competed for Linda's attention, while making complete fools of themselves in the process. Later, Linda remarked to me sadly that she felt her wedding was ruined by their inappropriate public behavior.

In Linda's unhappy situation, her parents were unwilling to call a truce even for their own daughter. They exhibited childish behavior that damaged their image in the eyes of others and caused irreparable damage to the relationships they had with their daughter. As we establish our new separate lives, animosity and anger between former spouses generally decreases, if we are willing to let it go.

A newly divorced engineer from San Francisco who had a difficult time forgiving his former wife, began to bless his partner in prayer. He commented to me: "Within days I began to feel peace and sincere blessings for her. Surprisingly, as my attitude changed, so did hers, generating a more sensible, calm working relationship as we co-parent our daughter." Still another friend, after the sting of divorce subsided, reported:

> I know she did not leave me just to hurt me. She was unhappy in the marriage and felt she would grow to hate me. In her perception, divorce was the only way to avoid that. Now I understand and accept her in that decision and forgive the hurt that resulted.

As Christians we believe that God, in unconditional love and acceptance of each of us, forgives us regardless of what we do and leads us through Jesus to love and forgive others. Jesus gives us examples of this kind of compassion and forgiveness in his parables, especially in the story of the prodigal son, also called the parable of the forgiving father. In an article in *Notre Dame Magazine* on this parable, James Burtchaell, CSC, wrote:

> The story is not really about the young son; the main character is the father. . . . The ruined and desperate son heads home not because he is repentant but because he is starving. The story never suggests that he has had a change of heart; only a change of diet. He is still the same schlemiel of a son who comes scuffing up the road to the homestead. The father has been waiting, watching, wishing. He does not let the son get to the porch, but runs to meet him. He interrupts his prepared job-hunting speech, sweeps him into his embrace, and orders a household celebration.[2]

Jesus further exemplifies forgiveness of deep hurt and injustice when he says during his own painful agony of the cross, "Forgive them, Father! They don't know what they are doing" (Lk 23:34). Through prayer, we can accept this unconditional forgiveness for ourselves and extend it to those who hurt us, even former spouses who may continue to unsettle our lives.

I have often thought a religious ritual might encourage forgiveness and peaceful closure on a failed marriage. Because of anger and bitterness, such a ceremony may not be possible for many divorcing couples. For those who might welcome such an opportunity, however, the private ritual might occur like this:

> The separating family comes to express their sorrow to each other, their children, and God at the death of the marriage.
>
> After an introduction and opening prayer, the priest or spiritual leader selects a passage from scripture on forgiveness and healing for a brief homily.
>
> Then the leader prays over the family a prayer of healing, acceptance, and peace. Parents pray for each other and their children and make promises to keep their legal and moral agreements and obligations toward the children and each other.
>
> The leader signs a cross in oil on each member of the family symbolizing God's unconditional forgiveness and love. Together all say the Our Father and give each other a sign of peace.

A final blessing on all as they go forth to pursue a new separate life concludes the brief ceremony.

Such a ritual assures the children that both parents still love and care for them and that they are free to love both parents without repercussions. It also offers the divorcing couple an opportunity to replace anger and guilt with growing acceptance and peaceful closure on the past, engendering freedom to begin anew.

Previous Marital History

When we enter into a new relationship that evolves into marriage, the past marriage remains a part of our adult history. Sometimes that memory — a ghost from the past — affects our present or future actions. Also, the behavior of our present spouse can remind us of the negative behavior of our former spouse to which we unconsciously react. In these situations, we must separate the present from the past so that we do not react inappropriately. Although human beings are more alike than different, we are not identical nor do we respond to all situations identically. If we pay attention to our reactions, we can avoid negative behavior based on past experiences.

For example, Carl, a musician from Philadelphia, spoke of his first brief marriage (less than six months) when he was in his twenties. Now, ten years later, the unhappy memory haunts him as he approaches his second marriage. He becomes cautious as old fears and past angers surface, and he questions whether he should take this marital step.

Betty, thirty-three, told of her explosive, unreasonable anger at her second husband upon his late arrival home from work, concluding, "Only later did I realize that my misplaced anger was rooted in my past marriage to a man whose constant tardiness was due to alcohol abuse."

During the years that follow the end of a first marriage, we may find ourselves at social functions with our former spouse. School parent meetings, birthdays, graduations, baptisms, weddings, funerals, and births of grandchildren do not cease because of divorce. One of the signs that the past has been accepted and put to rest is the ease with which we attend these activities with our new partner when our former spouse may be present. Trust, respect, and openness about the past in our current relationship sustains us so that these occasions do not become the source of undue jealousy or stress.

In some situations a chance meeting with a former spouse could be explosive and therefore should be avoided. When unavoidable, former partners usually maintain a cool, respectful distance. The following two examples show how dis-ease with the past and jealousy can interfere in a second marriage.

> Don, remarried, feels so strongly about not mixing his past with his new life that he refuses to attend any family function at which his first wife and her new husband might be present. Other family members and the couple in question are reasonably comfortable on those rare occasions and no problems occur. However, due to Don's fears, family members must plan separate gatherings so Don and his present wife will not encounter his first wife and her present husband.

> Julie, divorced after a twenty-year marriage, remarried within a year. The second marriage ended in divorce because of the inability of her second partner to accept her past, or any reminders of it. His jealousy of her friends and family reached the point that he monitored her phone calls. Though they loved each other, they were unable to resolve this conflict and the marriage disintegrated.

As you prepare for a second marriage, you and your partner need to explore your feelings regarding your past histories and develop ways in which you can comfortably speak of your past. You also need a positive outlook so you can live with the "past" persons who will continue to be a part of your present and future, especially if there are children involved.

Karen and Roger, another remarried couple from California, have satisfactorily blended the past with the present within their respective families. Karen's grown children, grandchildren, former in-laws, and friends accept Roger without question. Roger also feels welcome and enjoys the family gatherings. In addition, Roger's first wife still actively participates in his family and both she and Karen often enjoy his family's hospitality together without rancor or ill will. Karen says: "I do not want to interfere with Betsy's close ties with his family. Yet, as Roger's present wife, I have formed my own relationship with the family that is mutually satisfying."

Because of the openness and flexibility of these individuals and their maturity, confidence, and sense of self-worth, each sees their relationship with their respective families as unique and acceptable. Moreover, each family also respects and loves the new spouses without withdrawing the love they have for the former partners.

As we put peaceful closure on the past, we recognize the great resource our first marriage can be in preparation for a second union. We discover some insights that assist us in understanding our own needs and wants. The following five questions may be helpful in discovering these insights.

1. What have I learned about myself and my past marriage through the divorce?

2. What good qualities of my past marriage do I want in a future marriage?

3. What experiences of the past marriage do I want to eliminate from any future relationship?

4. What goals and expectations do I have about marriage?

5. What important qualities do I look for in a mate?

One final reminder for second marrieds: although it may be tempting, do not verbally compare your spouses. When you notice differences, especially negative ones, keep them to yourself or it may create havoc in your new relationship. Accept and cherish your new partner as the unique individual he or she is, rather than how you want him or her to be, especially in reference to your former spouse.

Communication and Anger

Communication is a loving gift given and received. To share one's fears and deepest feelings requires great trust in the listener. That kind of risky sharing is a precious gift given to the other. The receiver, when he or she listens with the heart, without interruption, judgment, criticism, or premature interpretation, shows respect for the speaker's gift and returns a treasured gift of supportive listening. Those couples who recognize the giftedness of good communication greatly enhance their intimacy and love.

Divorced persons, painfully aware of the lack of communication in their failed marriages, want to become better communicators. Couples want to share their fears and hidden insecurities candidly, and they ask to be heard and accepted unconditionally. They want to resolve conflicts satisfactorily.

One troublesome area in communication is the expression of frustration and anger. To resolve conflicts, each person needs to understand how he or she expresses anger and even examine how anger was conveyed through the childhood family history. Frequently, the role-modeling of our parents and any unwritten rules about angry behavior are significant to understanding our own feelings or behavior in anger.

Some people immediately explode in anger; then, after calming down, they are willing to work at resolving the conflict. Others silently sulk, requiring space and quiet time to work out confusing emotions before discussion. Still others, fearful of anger and being out of control, or afraid of being rejected or abandoned, suppress their angry feelings. Some, out of touch with their emotions, contend they are not angry, yet their tone of voice and body language belies them. Individuals frequently and unconsciously mask their anger in guilt and depression. Anger can smoulder beneath the surface as a secret grudge until an attack can be directed at the person who is the object of the anger.

Like all feelings, anger is neither good nor bad, it just is. If, however, we ignore it or bury it, it builds up energy until we lash out inappropriately, sometimes hurting an innocent bystander. If we acknowledge our anger and uncover what is bothering us, we can defuse it and resolve the problem. Anger produces creative energy useful for developing methods to resolve conflicts.

Listening

Perhaps the greatest key to good communication and diffusing anger is a caring, respectful listener. If I risk sharing who I am with my partner, even in anger, and he or she disregards, criticizes, or withholds support, I may never risk trusting that person again. A good listening friend:

- ♦ considers the other's point of view;
- ♦ listens respectfully without interruption;
- ♦ listens for the underlying emotions expressed;
- ♦ does not mentally prepare defensive arguments while listening to others;
- ♦ helps clarify frustrated feelings, so that one stops venting emotion and begins to solve the problem.

Good listening offers us the opportunity to grow and understand ourselves better as we grow closer to our listening partner. We all have strengths and weaknesses. When we help each other with the loving gift of supportive listening and reflecting feelings, and share the burdens of our weaknesses, we become strong.

Inevitably, couples experience differences in marriage and quarrel. When such a crisis occurs, we can view the conflict as an opportunity to respond creatively to a problem and negotiate change. Furthermore, each experience of creative resolution strengthens us to tackle future crises successfully. Differences left unresolved fester and frequently become the seeds of destruction in the marriage. Too often, individuals see conflict as competition, a power struggle of right and wrong. The need to "win" the argument takes precedence over solving the problem.

One couple I know started early in their marriage to talk of their dreams and plans for their lives together as well as their individual needs. They also risked sharing some trouble spots in their relationship. Sometimes, in the heat of their discussions, they structured their speaking time with a timer so that each could express their feelings without interruption. The receiver listened without mentally forming a defense, and when the problem was satisfactorily stated, they negotiated acceptable changes.

Many psychologists and teachers of communication skills suggest that when conflict becomes highly emotional and competitive, we need a structure that will allow us to negotiate change. Apparently, this is one of the primary uses of Robert's Rules of Order in business meetings. Although a structured process appears frustrating and time-consuming to an impatient person in the throes of anger, it actually opens up the possibility for consensus and acceptable change. The structured process suggested below can assist people in various types of relationships to negotiate a resolution to a conflict in such a way that both parties feel satisfied and validated.

A. Set a specific time and time limit to discuss the problem. Set the following guidelines:

   ♦ Place and time convenient to both parties.

   ♦ No outside interruptions.

   ♦ No drugs or alcohol during discussion.

   ♦ Stick to the current topic, no history of past disappointments.

   ♦ Set speaking time limits, no interruptions.

   ♦ Maintain good eye contact.

B. Define the problem.

   ♦ The one who experiences the problem makes "I" statements: "When _____ happens, I feel _____."

   ♦ The listening partner reflects back to the speaking partner the feelings and words he or she heard (the heart of the message) without judgment or criticism: "Are you saying that you feel _____ because _____?" or "It sounds like you feel _____ when _____ happens."

   ♦ When both parties agree on what the problems and feelings are, they can begin to explore possibilities for resolution.

C. Develop solutions.

   ♦ Brainstorm by listing all possibilities on paper, without judgment or criticism, even if they seem impractical, impossible, or ridiculous. (This can be fun!)

   ♦ Look at responsibilities/consequences of each suggestion, prioritize in order of preference, and choose one that both are willing to try.

   ♦ Determine a limited try-out time and time for evaluation.

   ♦ In closing, touch or hug and express your gratitude for this common effort.

D. Evaluate the solution.

   ♦ Determine the effectiveness of the tried solution: did it work and how do each of you feel about it?

♦ If solution was ineffective or unsatisfactory, review alternatives and follow the same procedure until the problem is resolved.

E. Congratulate yourselves on creatively resolving your problem and celebrate your reconciliation!

Important Notes About Quarreling

♦ Honesty, respect, kindness, tact, and the intent to negotiate a solution rather than win the argument strengthen the possibility of resolution.

♦ Recognize that when one has a problem, both do because it affects the relationship.

♦ Talk in terms of "How can *we* solve this problem?" or "How can I help?"

♦ Whenever the session deteriorates into a shouting, blaming match, call a cooling-off period and set a new appointment. Do not leave arguments unfinished.

♦ Avoid statements such as "you always" or "you never." Speak your own feelings by saying, "I feel . . ."

♦ Avoid physical abuse and "below-the-belt punches" — those ugly, retaliatory, belittling remarks that strike at your partner's weaknesses. These only add fuel to the argument, destroying chances for a satisfactory resolution. One thirty-year-old psychologist said, "Anytime anyone calls me stupid, I become so emotionally incensed that any further work at resolving an argument is impossible until I have calmed down."

♦ Avoid unfair tactics.

♦ Avoid arguing in public or serious arguments in front of the children.

♦ Admit your own wrong by saying "I'm sorry."

♦ Forgive and forget. Once the matter is resolved, do not use it against your partner at a later time.

♦ Whenever possible, maintain a sense of humor.

Lisa and Jim began using a procedure such as this after many years of marriage. They found it so useful, and the brainstorming so much fun, that they have successfully resolved some of their long-standing disagreements.

Whenever Ted and Alice reach a serious impasse over an important problem, they wisely decide to seek some professional assistance from their friend and counselor for clarification. Usually, they need only one session to put the issue back into perspective, so that they can negotiate a mutually acceptable solution.

Unresolved serious problems simmer beneath the surface, building energy and collecting fuel through additional perceived injuries in the relationship. Eventually the pressure triggers an explosion, which, in some unhappy situations leads to irreparable damage resulting in divorce.

Reconciliation

Apologies and forgiveness are an integral part of any loving relationship. Whether intentionally or not, we all occasionally hurt others. When partners resolve conflict satisfactorily, they reconcile the relationship through their forgiveness of past hurts and their apologies for their own contribution to the problem. The good feelings of peacefulness, self-esteem, and intimacy that ensue certainly call for a celebration of the reconciliation, which should not be neglected. The joyful celebration builds a couple's power-base and renews their lifelong commitment to each other.

Larry and I received a special gift on our wedding day, a pottery goblet accompanied with the following note, signed by our friends Louie and Maureen:

> The cup for centuries has been passed among those who share trust, love, vision. Men have raised the cup to celebrate joy, dreams, hope — life! At those special times in your life together may this cup be a celebration symbol. . . . And, if ever harsh words or bitter feelings should come between you, let one of you be the first to fill the cup and take it to the other that you may both drink deeply. . . .

Larry and I have used this cup several times in forgiveness as well as in celebration. Because we see the cup as a symbol of the core of our relationship — the love that bonds us together — we highly value its significance. When one of us brings the cup to the other to break the impasse or silence, the other accepts and drinks from it. To refuse the cup means that we refuse to value the loving commitment we made to each other in the sacrament of marriage. Neither of us, regardless of how angry or upset we feel at times, are willing to abandon that shared love. In accepting the cup, we open communication once again. With apologies and forgiveness as our starting point, we then negotiate a satisfactory solution to our disagreement.

Conclusion

Couples who value their loving commitment to each other strive to eliminate unnecessary bitterness and rancor from their life, whether it comes from past marital partners and history or present occurrences. They recognize that all lovers argue occasionally. They know that it takes love, trust, perseverance, and prayer to manage conflict, and that it takes forgiveness to avoid the irreparable consequences of past hurts. They view apologies and forgiveness as gifts given and received in relationship through the graces of the sacrament of marriage. Above all, they want to nourish and deepen their love for each other and rely on the inherent strength of this sacrament to assist them in their endeavor.

In her poem "Love," Barb Upham offers her insights on loving relationships:

Love takes time.
It needs a history of giving and receiving, laughing and
    crying. . . .
Love never promises instant gratification, only ultimate
    fulfillment.
Love means believing in someone, in something.
It supposes a willingness to struggle, to work, to suffer, and to
    rejoice.
Satisfaction and ultimate fulfillment are by-products of
    dedicated love.
They belong only to those who can reach beyond themselves;
to whom giving is more important than receiving.
Love is doing everything you can to help others build
    whatever dreams they have.
Love involves much careful and active listening.

It is doing whatever needs to be done, and saying whatever
will promote the other's happiness, security, and well-being.
Sometimes, love hurts.
Love is on a constant journey to what others need.
It must be attentive, caring, and open, both to what others
say and to what others cannot say. . . .
Love says no with empathy and great compassion.
Love is firm, but when needed it must be tender.
When others have tried and failed,
love is the hand in yours in your moments of discouragement
and disappointment.
Love is reliable.
Love is a choice and commitment to others' true and lasting
happiness.
It is dedicated to growth and fulfillment.
Love is not selfish.
Love sometimes fails for lack of wisdom or abundance of
weakness,
but it forgives, knowing the intentions are good.
Love does not attach conditions. . .
genuine love is always a free gift.
Love realizes and accepts that there will be disagreements and
disturbing emotions. . . .
There may be times when miles lay between, but love is a
commitment.
It believes and endures all things.
Love encourages freedom of self.
Love shares positive and negative reactions to warm and cold
feelings.
Love, intimate love, will never reject others.
It is the first to encourage and the last to condemn.
Love is a commitment to growth, happiness, and fulfillment
of one another.[3]

— Barb Upham

Former Marital History / Conflict
WORKSHEET

Privately answer the questions, or respond to the statements with *Agree* or *Disagree*. Then share with your partner.

1. In examining my past marriage relationship, what were the weaknesses — those things which I do not want to experience again?

2. What were the strengths — those things I would like in my present or future relationships?

3. What were the weaknesses/strengths of my former spouse or partner?

4. In objective retrospect, what were the contributing factors to the marital failure?

5. How did I contribute to that failure? My former partner?

6. Am I able to forgive my former spouse for his/her share in that failure?

7. Am I able to forgive myself for my share in that failure?

8. Have I let go of the anger, bitterness, and hurt from the past?

9. Is there any unfinished business from my former marriage that needs to be resolved? Any resentments or regrets?

10. If so, what steps have I taken or can take to complete the process toward resolution?

11. Are there some problems about my former marriage that may never be resolved?

12. What have I learned from my past experience of marriage and divorce?

13. Am I really ready to put the past behind me and move forward with confidence?

14. I need a marriage partner in order to be happy.

15. Define happiness, friendship, love.

16. I accept the way my partner handles his/her problems.

17. Two problems I foresee us having are . . .

18. I will do anything I can to avoid disagreement with my partner.

19. When I am angry, I say or do hurtful things to my partner.

20. Some of the subjects we argue about are . . .

21. We should never quarrel.

22. I never feel angry.

23. How did I express anger as a child? How do I now?

24. I am afraid of feeling angry.

25. I deal with my feelings of anger in the following ways . . .

26. We should always keep our anger under control.

27. I avoid conflict or disagreements with my partner by . . .

28. It is all right to yell, cry, curse, or call each other names during a quarrel.

29. Physical abuse is never acceptable in a marital relationship.

30. Too often my partner refuses to bend on a particular issue(s).

31. One of us always has to be right.

32. When we have offended each other, my partner refuses to talk about it.

33. I do not like the way my partner expresses anger.

34. When we argue we should not bring up grievances from the past.

35. Define hostility, aggression, anger.

36. When I am angry, I need time alone to sort things out before I can work on the problem.

37. When I am angry, I need to express it explosively right away to relieve stress, so that I can more easily work on the problem later.

38. If I experience a problem in our relationship, I should try to resolve it myself.

39. If I tell my partner what I feel, he/she won't love me, will be angry, and will reject me.

40. I do not like my partner to run away in the middle of a quarrel.

41. I want my partner to apologize after an argument.

42. I find it hard to say "I am sorry" when I am wrong.

43. When we disagree on major issues, we should turn to an experienced professional for help.

44. I am open to getting marital counseling if we find our marriage is floundering.

45. In order to be happy, we should agree on everything.

Additional Comments:

Deep peace of the Running Wave to you.
Deep peace of the Flowing Air to you.
Deep peace of the Quiet Earth to you.
Deep peace of the Shining Stars to you.
Deep peace of the Son of Peace to you.

— *Celtic Benediction*

CHAPTER 3

Creating
a Stepfamily

A stepfamily is born of many losses. Family members have different histories and expectations. Parent-child relationships predate the relationship of the new couple. An influential biological parent exists elsewhere in actuality or in memory. Children may be members of two or more households. Legal relationships are ambiguous or nonexistent.[1]

> — Ann Getzoff and Carolyn McClenahan
> *Step Kids: A Survival Guide for*
> *Teenagers in Stepfamilies*

Stepfamily life is filled with unexpected twists and turns that drain the emotional resources of the merging families. To merge two families successfully requires flexibility, loving patience, tough negotiating skills, and a sense of humor.

In courtship, individuals choose one another, adjusting to and accommodating each other as they draw closer in love. In contrast, the children do not choose their stepparents or any accompanying stepsiblings, nor do they have much opportunity to develop a loving bond with those new people entering their family life. In essence, the marriage is imposed on the children of both parties.

It is also important to note that second marriages are born out of a loss, whether it be the death of a partner or the death of a relationship. Adjustments are painful both for adults and for children. When a single parent family forms after such a loss, the bond between parent and child intensifies. Parents and children rely on each other for support and consult each other about family activities such as vacations, eating out, or movies. When a second marriage occurs, the children are pushed to the edge of the parent-child relationship as the new spouse takes his or her rightful place in forming the couple bond. Children experience a second loss when they lose the close relationship they had with their parent, and they compete with the new stepparent for the love and attention of the biological parent.

Parents often expect their children to accept and even love their new spouse almost immediately, when, in fact, the children may feel angry and guilty while still grieving over the break-up of their original family. Often, they resent another family change, especially having to accept someone else as a new parental authority figure. Furthermore, in the case of divorce, remarriage extinguishes the cherished hope that mommy and daddy will get back together again and frequently ignites the fear that the absent parent's love will be lost to the children forever. Children may also dislike the stepparent or one or more of the stepsiblings. Such conflicting feelings often result in children "acting out" as they wonder who loves them and where they really do belong.

Stepparents also enter the second marriage expecting to love their partner's children as much as their own, then feel guilty when they discover their persistent partiality to their own children. Instant love is a myth. Parents bond with their children tightly through a long history of loving care, communication, problem-solving, and instinct. In contrast, stepparents step into a family history and must begin immediately to communicate and problem-solve with strangers. Bonding comes later.

Because stepfamilies do not naturally form the "Brady Bunch," family therapy can prepare the ground for the marriage. A few counseling sessions before the marriage offer an opportunity for all members of the new family-to-be to express conflicting feelings of fear, love, anger, confusion, and insecurity. Voicing potential problems and unrealistic expectations provides an occasion for creative resolution. Developing awareness of the responsibilities and challenges of stepfamily living better prepares the couple for those early months of their new marriage.

Some of the problems that challenge stepfamilies are: acceptance, divided loyalties, territory, weekend children, discipline, family traditions, sexual tensions, and having children in common.

Acceptance

Initially, most children resist accepting new people into their existing family structure, just as the body resists a transplanted organ. Some children may appear comfortable with a parent's dating friend but when marriage occurs, hostile behavior often surfaces. Children, like all of us, prefer the status quo and can stage effective sabotage to resist change. The greatest battle frequently comes from the adolescent who is already in the natural stages of separation from family.

Stepparents frequently comment on the fact that in the beginning, stepchildren can walk into a room and immediately connect with their natural parent while ignoring the presence of the stepparent. Most stepparents find this type of behavior unacceptable, and the natural parent doesn't always understand the experience or is at a loss to remedy the situation. One stepparent told us of his experience with his stepson:

> In the beginning, my stepson, Hal, would stop a conversation in mid-sentence and walk out of the room whenever I entered. It was as if I didn't exist. I felt angry and inadequate and very much an outsider. In time, we all got some counseling and now Hal and I are developing a respectful relationship. If my wife hadn't been understanding of my feelings, I would have left the marriage.

Younger and even adult children can cause significant problems. The example below illustrates a child's struggle to accept a new, permanent adult in his home.

> For the past six years, Mary, a single parent, has relied on her responsible teen-age son, Allen, for emotional support and household help. When Lewis entered Mary's life and the relationship blossomed, Allen acted jealous, protecting his mother and defending his own status. He resented stepping aside to allow another man to be the new adult male in his mother's life and a new parental authority figure in his own. He resisted the wedding. Lewis, respecting Allen's long-standing place in the home, wisely decided to approach Allen slowly, as an adult friend rather than a heavy-handed parent. Though Mary had misgivings about his approach, she did not interfere. Their caution resulted in Allen and Lewis mutually accepting and respecting each other within eighteen months.

Adult children, already out of the family home and living on their own or married with their own families also have concerns when a parent remarries, especially after the family has been divided by a painful divorce. Some worry about promised inheritances. Others become concerned about a parent giving more to the new spouse than he or she did to the divorced or deceased spouse. Some find the new spouse intrusive in their lives, especially when the parent seems to push the new spouse onto the family. Some adult children refuse to deal with the issue at all and keep a distance from the parent and new spouse altogether.

My three adult sons—two newly married — were in their mid-twenties when I remarried. I was aware of their cautious approach to my second marriage, but no problems developed. Recently, when I asked my sons how they had felt when I remarried, they listed the following concerns that they had discussed with each other:

♦ Is it too soon for mom to marry? Will mom be happy? Is she over dad? Will it last? We don't want her to go through another traumatic, painful divorce.

♦ Will they be compatible since Larry is different than dad?

♦ What are his motives? Can we trust him to be good to mom and not take advantage of her emotionally or financially?

♦ How should we relate to him? He's never had kids. Do we have to relate to him as a stepfather? Will he expect us to treat him like a father? What should we call him? What will he expect of us? Will we have any obligations toward him once he is married to mom?

My sons soon became comfortable with Larry because he didn't place any expectations on them and did not push for any relationship. It was difficult for him to walk into such a close-knit family, but since he came from one himself, he patiently allowed the relationships to take their natural course. My sons also allowed time for a friendship to develop. I told them that they needed to respect Larry as they would any other person and respect him as my husband, but they did not have to be friends if they did not choose to. Gradually they got to know and accept one another, and Larry is an accepted family member now. The anxiety lingered in one son, however. As his own children began to call Larry "grandpa" he felt very uncomfortable. I suspect that came from his own feelings of disloyalty to his father in allowing this to happen. Those feelings subsided as he discovered that his friendship with Larry did not threaten his love for his father and that the children were lucky to have an extra grandfather who loved them.

Divided Loyalties

Initially, a child may react angrily toward the stepparent out of fear that in showing acceptance or love to the stepparent the child betrays the love for his or her natural parent, who, in turn, will angrily withdraw love from the child. Children need assurance that the stepparent is not replacing the absent parent — is not a new "daddy" or "mommy." Children truly want to be loved by everyone, but will need time to discover that love is complete and different with each person, that it is a quality of relationship without quantitative value, and that love for one person does not diminish the love for another. Primarily, children need to feel loved by both biological parents and need to be free to love and have access to both parents without interference, recriminations, or guilt. Those children who maintain a healthy, loving relationship with both natural parents remain emotionally more stable than those who are denied access to one parent or are used as pawns or spies between two embittered parents.

Gino and Sally discovered a method to help Jessica, Sally's seven-year-old daughter, cope with the confusion of the two "daddies" in her life. On one of Jessica's birthdays, Gino spontaneously signed his card, "Daddy #2." Jessica loved it and subsequently responded to this distinction by addressing cards and gifts and referring to Gino as Daddy #2. Gino explains:

> She seemed at ease with this distinction, for this label relieved her of trying to cope with the confusing dilemma of two daddies. She still calls me Gino, not daddy, but when speaking to others, I am Daddy #2. Although her natural father is primary, I know I am also important to her.

Sometimes stepparents notice stepchildren "watching" them as if from a distance. While "watching," the child discovers what behavior is expected and acceptable to this new parental figure. The child also learns about the different kinds of care involved and how to keep all his or her love relationships in balance.

Territory

In the new family, members must learn to share living space, family income, family obligations, family time, and family affection. Consequently, each person needs to be willing to make physical and psychological space for additional family members. A child may resent having to share a formerly private room with a sibling or stepsibling. The parent's bedroom, which may have been accessible to the children in the past, may now be off limits because of the privacy needs of the newly married couple. The child's birth-order place in the family most likely will be challenged and changed. The youngest of one parent may become the middle child in the new family structure or the oldest may become the youngest. The change in numbers affects the family also. An only child may acquire instant brothers and/or sisters, or a family of one or two teenagers may increase to several young people, all competing for a place of belonging in the family while at the same time striving for their emancipation and independence. Even a parent becomes territory and sharing mom or dad with another adult, let alone other children, traumatizes some youngsters.

Territory also includes the house and yard, as Martin, forty-five, ruefully explains: "I was trimming some bushes out in the yard one day, when my hostile stepson confronted me with the caustic remark, 'We don't trim our bushes that way. We like the natural look!'"

Another middle-aged friend, George, speaks of joining his one-child family with Alice's three children, all four teenagers. The change in the food bill and the customs that each family had developed around the ritual of eating generated some major problems.

"My sixteen-year-old quarterback son and his friends," says George, "could eat their way through the house in a matter of minutes, like carpenter ants. Her kids were quiet, polite, creative, and small eaters! At breakfast when they went for the cereal, it was gone. My son had finished it with a quart of milk as a midnight snack the night before. During the week's shopping, I bought separate boxes of cereal for each of her children, and three or four for my son.

"At the table when food was passed, her children politely took one serving, leaving seconds for later — but, there weren't any seconds left because my son had taken first and second servings on his first round. Her children were free to take their meals to their rooms if they didn't want to sit with us. My son had always been expected to eat at the table with the family and then clear his plate when finished."

Shrugging his shoulders, George continued, "We tried to organize TV-watching, chores, use of the bathroom, morning showers, and laundry times. No matter what schedule we tried, nothing worked. Chaos ruled the household most of the time. Nobody wanted to give up territory or change past routines, and each, including my wife and I, jealously guarded our own and our children's territories. We finally called it quits."

An important area of territory sometimes overlooked is the need of the non-custodial visiting children for a place of their own. To set aside a permanent drawer or closet space and, if possible, a bed for these children helps them feel that they belong and are not outsiders. During their absence, these territorial areas remind others of their membership in the family and assures the returning children of their place in their parent's home. Furthermore, successful stepfamilies recommend that couples integrate non-custodial children into the household by giving them tasks and responsibilities and not treating them as guests.

Weekend Children

The complex arrangements of "weekend children" present special problems for the stepfamily. Families expand and contract week to week, even day to day. Determining "who will be home when" challenges even the best of nuclear families, let alone the stepfamily with custodial and non-custodial children. The confusing, disruptive, and sometimes overwhelming situation often causes parents to wonder who is in the family and who is not. Consequently, they may question the wisdom of the remarriage.

Furthermore, couples speak of the behavioral changes of children at the beginning or ending of visits and the stress it causes all concerned. These children readjust to each household weekly and must respond differently as well as follow different rules. They may feel angry about this life of see-saw changes and act out as they switch back and forth between families. Some families allow the child to spend some time alone with the biological parent when they first arrive or prepare to leave. Others state that providing a few hours of quiet time helps the child to withdraw from one family and to ease back into another.

Carlos, an engineer, and his wife Maryanne, a legal secretary, live in Texas; each has three children by previous marriages. Maryanne's three teens live with them but visit their father every other weekend. Carlos shares joint physical custody with his former spouse, who lives nearby. His eight-year-old, ten-year-old, and fourteen-year-old visit on alternating weeks from Sundays to Wednesdays, or Wednesdays to Sundays. Their schedule is further complicated by the children's busy round of school, sports, and social activities.

> "It has been almost a year since our wedding," complains Maryanne, "and I still can't get used to this unreal schedule. We keep a master calendar in the kitchen but there are so many last minute changes, I sometimes feel I want out of this craziness." With tears brimming in her eyes, she adds, "You know, I can't even remember the last time Carlos and I had a weekend together, alone."

In such cases, it is imperative that the couple share and listen to each other's feelings and develop some creative coping strategies, such as spending special time alone together before the arrival of children, or arranging for car pools. Seeking outside support and professional help to alleviate the obvious strain may also be necessary. As couples struggle together through crisis to a successful conclusion, they can bond more closely and develop a sense of "we-ness" rather than a feeling of individual isolation. Consequently, their joint problem solving becomes the success mechanism that motivates them to try again in the face of future problems. Unfortunately, however, if this kind of stress is ignored and not resolved, it can — and, as statistics indicate, often does — lead to marital burn-out.

Discipline

Discipline styles of remarrying partners may be incompatible. When we first marry and have children, we have time to prepare and discuss how we plan to raise our children. Through trial and error, we develop a family lifestyle and discipline patterns as our families grow. With the creation of a stepfamily, past imprinted individual patterns may clash, especially if the shift is from permissive to strict. Teens, particularly, resist changes at the time of their own growing independence and can be formidable opponents to any new efforts to control them. Discussing child-rearing strategies and discipline styles before marriage can alleviate some problems before they establish a stronghold.

In *Dealing With Discipline, A Stepfamily Living Booklet*, authors Linda Albert and Elizabeth Einstein outline three common styles of discipline: autocratic — the boss; permissive — servant or bystander; and democratic — leader, guide or coach.[2] They strongly recommend that stepfamilies adopt the democratic style to accommodate the past histories of the family members and to avoid a continual power struggle between adults and children. It is especially suited to stepfamily living because children cooperate best when they participate in the family structuring and governing. Parents, stepparents, and children work together to establish consistent rules and routines and to set consequences and limits for behavior.

The democratic approach contributes to a relaxed, orderly, and consistent home atmosphere. It also affords the family an opportunity to plan their recreational activities and set family goals. In addition, the democratic approach fosters growth in self-esteem, self-discipline, and responsibility. The authors also remind readers that since most adults were not raised in the democratic style, they may need some assistance in developing the appropriate skills. Resources are found in parenting workshops and publications readily available in most communities at a reasonable cost.

Psychologist Jane Nelsen, Ed.D., in her book *Positive Discipline*, recommends the democratic approach of regular "family meetings" to ease some of the stress all families encounter.[3] She warns parents, however, not to use these meetings as another place to issue directives. The message of love must get through. In a family meeting, each person freely expresses needs, wants, and concerns. All members, even the youngest ones, may suggest family rules, household responsibilities, discipline, family outings and activities, and future goals. As problems develop, they can be resolved in these gatherings. Nelsen also emphasizes that verbalized appreciations of each other should be included. Through this cooperative effort, family members accept more personal responsibility for family harmony, thus strengthening family relationships.

This highly structured process appears cumbersome at first and family members may resist. Change is not easy, but it is essential to the growth of family unity. If a commitment to a six-month trial period of regularly scheduled meetings is followed, the rewards of mutual cooperation and respect will bless the effort.

Few stepchildren will accept parental authority from a new stepparent during those first months of stepfamily living, especially adolescents, who often view the stepparent as an intruder. Our friend Stacy told us of her experience with her new husband's fifteen-year-old daughter:

> When I confronted Debbie, Sean's daughter, about doing the dinner dishes one night soon after we were married, she screamed at me, "I didn't do dishes in my old life, and I'm not about to do them in this life!" Exasperated, I thought to myself, "How about trying for your next life!"

The natural parent should take the lead in the parenting and discipline of his or her children, even if the couple decides to introduce the democratic family meeting approach to their family. The stepparent should offer follow-up support of the natural parent when working with the children. For example, "Your mother (father) said to . . ." or "We agreed at our family meeting that . . ." When there are differences between the two adults regarding discipline, an effective stepparent does not openly interfere in front of the children. The couple should resolve these inconsistencies privately — keeping fairness to all children in mind — so that in the presence of the children the couple presents a united front, and discipline is not undermined by either adult.

As with most children, building their self-esteem, treating them with respect, fairness, and consistency in discipline works effectively, especially if this approach is coupled with helping children take responsibility and experience the natural or logical consequences of their own misbehavior. Training in good parenting skills along with some stepfamily support and occasional outside therapy for trouble spots, will assist families to establish an acceptable stepfamily lifestyle. Such training is usually available through adult education programs in the local community.

In addition to the complexity of establishing discipline in the new family, the possibility of interference from the past, through absent parents, grandparents, or other interested extended family members presents itself. Guilt and angry feelings surface in a parent or stepparent when a child says, "In my dad's (mom's) house I don't have to..." or "Mom (Dad) lets me...buys me..." and so on. At such times, adults can stress that the rules of one household do not depend on the rules of another. Each household needs to maintain its autonomy.

Another common retort from stepchildren is: "You're not my mother (father). I don't have to do what you tell me." A good response might be, "You're right. I am not your real parent, but I am head of this household with your mom (dad) and I do care about your welfare. While you live here (or visit) you must follow the rules of this home."

Sometimes, natural parents successfully co-parent on major growth and educational development directions for their children. However, shared-parenting can occasionally be used by one adult as a wedge of control unless the family lines of demarcation are maintained. When relationships between the adults — parents and stepparents — are stable and respectful, all adults can develop acceptable family rules that will apply in all households, thus providing additional stability and consistency for the children regardless of where they are staying.

Non-Parent Partners

In some remarriages, only one partner is a parent. Often these non-parent partners feel hurt and angry as their initial efforts at loving care and parenting of stepchildren are rejected with apathetic or hostile behavior. Because a stepparent can rarely challenge the primary, long-term bond between parent and child, the child becomes the only one who, by attitude and behavior, allows the stepparent the privilege and permission to parent him or her.

Children can and often do bond with other adults, but it takes time for the bonding of trust and love to develop. Younger children, from infancy to eight years, will be more likely to accept a stepparent than older children, especially teens. However, stepparents can strive, without pushing, for friendship with stepchildren and, if in time children return acceptance and love to them as an alternate parent, it should be respected and valued as a special gift. Later, in their adult years, stepchildren often apologize to stepparents for their past angry, rejecting misbehavior, and gratefully respond to their stepparent's positive contributions to their lives.

Another concern of these non-parent remarrieds is the jealousy they feel when their partner spends time with his or her children. Even though intellectually the non-parent spouse understands the stronger, long-standing bond between parent and child, the irrational feelings of jealousy still surface. Rose and Gene, newly married, spoke of this difficulty with his elementary-school-age children.

> Gene began: "For a Christmas present, I planned to take my three children on a ski trip for a few days. I wanted Rose to come with us."
>
> Rose interrupted: "Yes, but I thought about it and decided not to go because I really don't like the snow. I thought it would be nice for Gene to have some time alone with his kids. However, a few hours after he left, I began to really miss him, then feel jealous and resentful that he was with them and I was alone, even though it was my choice."
>
> Gene continued: "Four days later, when the kids and I returned, I found Rose cold and angry and felt very confused. After returning the kids to their mother, we talked about our reactions."
>
> "Both of us were surprised about my unexpected reaction to this incident," added Rose. "Gene reassured me that he loved me and that I do come first in his life. We also concluded that our trips, with or without kids, would be to places we both enjoy."

Another couple, Maria and Ben, married for four years, have a different experience. They each have adult children, but they have been raised very differently. Marie commented:

> I resent the way Ben's children take advantage of him. The only time they call is to ask for money or help, and I am jealous of the way he bends over backwards for them, even though they rarely say thank-you or pay back their debts. They never call him just to say hello or ask him how he is. I feel for him when I see the hurt in his eyes after they treat him so shabbily.

My children treat both of us with respect. I would never allow my kids to be so irresponsible and callous, and I am disappointed in Ben when he lets his kids treat him so poorly. However, I'm resigned to accepting the situation and being more understanding and accepting of his love for his children.

Some non-parent partners cope with these intense feelings of jealousy and isolation by sharing their feelings, needs, and concerns with their partner. Caring spouses listen with empathy, understanding, and love. To relieve some of the pressure, couples plan special dates together, especially just before or after an encounter with the visiting children. The parent-spouse then makes every effort to bring the willing partner into activities and conversations with the children. Most couples who have successfully adjusted to stepfamily living indicate that it takes time, usually three or more years, for these fearful, angry emotions to give way to acceptance and love.

Rituals and Traditions

Unlike a first-marriage family, which gradually develops rituals and traditions to celebrate its story, the second-marriage family juggles many outside attachments and individuals moving in and out of the family circle. Natural parents, stepparents and stepchildren, grandparents, and assorted relatives and friends crowd this new family with their established traditions for births, graduations, weddings, holidays, and vacations. This total history impacts and overburdens the new stepfamily, especially the children.

Stepparents need to recognize and accept that living in this open-ended, crowded family is normal. Then, in the midst of this constant fluctuation, the new family must begin to create a history of its own, composed of the old and the new. The children's emotional and psychological health requires that some family traditions be maintained while new ones evolve. A family council offers the opportunity to consider possibilities that incorporate the immediate and extended family needs.

Christmas is probably the toughest holiday with which to cope because it involves so much personal history, memories, and expectations. It requires patience, flexibility, creative planning, and respect for individual traditions from stepfamily members. Because they shared no common history, one family selected a Christmas tradition from each family's past and created a new one of their own. Brainstorming together, they planned a special family day on the weekend before Christmas to see the lights and pageantry of San Francisco, followed by dinner at a favorite French restaurant. The children's Christmas was spent with other parents and/or grandparents, while the newly married couple took a much needed day for themselves.

Mark's stepfamily of seven, who have lived together in Oregon for four years, quarreled over trimming their first Christmas tree. Fifteen-year-old Mark said:

> Our first Christmas was a real bummer! Because we couldn't agree about anything, each half of our family took half the tree to decorate. We strung our side with cranberries and popcorn and added our homemade ornaments and speckled pine cones. My stepdad's family decorated with red and gold ornaments and tinsel. The tree looked pretty awful. We even set our presents on our side. The only thing we all liked was the little town of Bethlehem with the Christmas scene we put under the tree.
>
> On the second Christmas, we knew each other better and we decided to decorate together. Mom suggested that we draw names at Thanksgiving so that we could make a nice ornament for another family member. On Christmas Eve we opened them, hung them on the tree, and had the greatest time. I still have the cut-out yellow star with crayon scribbles that my stepsister, Carolyn, who was three, gave me. I thought it was pretty neat since she was so little. We had so much fun that we draw names every year now. It's our family's favorite Christmas activity.

It is also possible to look at traditions over a one or two year cycle to accommodate the needs of everyone. In our family, we alternate holidays among various family members. Thanksgiving may be with one set of grandparents, Christmas Eve for ourselves, Christmas Day at Dad's, Easter at Larry's and my home. Next year's plans will change as our family needs change. When it is impossible to meet everyone's needs on holidays, arrangements are made for visiting special others in advance or following the holiday. Some families prefer to visit friends regularly during the year instead of just during the holiday time. With so many more people involved in stepfamily life, the new family must prioritize their time to create their own history and traditions. Others will have to wait their turn. Flexibility and openness to the constant change in stepfamily living results in new and creative celebrations of the family history.

The Sexual Dimension

Three aspects of sexuality need to be recognized and addressed in a stepfamily: the sexuality of the honeymooning couple, the possible sexual attraction between teen stepchildren, and the possible sexual attraction between stepparent and stepchild.

Unlike first marrieds, who have the luxury of their honeymoon months to themselves, remarrieds with custody of one or more children must honeymoon in a crowd. Their freedom of sexual expression must be confined to a bedroom or a private room, and they may find that children's activities limit the time and frequency available for their sexual intimacy. They may have to curtail open affectionate gestures when children are present. Generally, these couples establish rules of knocking before entering, even installing locks on the inside of their bedroom doors to protect their privacy. One stepparent jokingly suggested that they put a sign on their bedroom door saying, "Don't knock unless you are bleeding!"

Tina, a busy mother of four and stepparent to two (five of whom are teens), spoke of the difficulty she and Jim had when they remarried six months ago and had to establish some new rules for their own privacy. Tina told me her story:

> Before I was remarried, there was an open door policy to my bedroom. Frequently my teen-agers came in after a date to share their good time or some of their concerns. Now that Jim and I are married, we close our bedroom door and the children must knock, and wait for a response, before entering. Because of a couple of surprise entrances, we also installed a lock on the door.
>
> It has been hard for the kids. At first they resented Jim's access to our bedroom, and were angry with me for closing the door on them. I want and need to be with Jim but I feel guilty about leaving them out and I also miss those special evening sharing times with my children. Now, however, they are more accepting of the situation, especially since I make time to be with them and sometimes

go into their rooms at night after they return from an evening out, just to check if they want to talk.

Other couples in similar situations make arrangements for their live-in children to visit their other natural parents, grandparents, or friends on occasional weekends so that they are free for intimate time together without interruption. Sometimes couples hire babysitters so they can get away for a few hours.

Teen-agers' budding sexual awareness and development, coupled with the sexually charged atmosphere of newly married adults, contribute to the second sexual concern of many stepfamilies: sexual attraction of some stepteens to each other. When stepsiblings grow up together from childhood, the brother/sister relationship naturally establishes itself and the incidence of stepsiblings becoming sexually active with each other is reduced. When teens are suddenly thrust into living together in the same household as a result of a remarriage, they can be overwhelmed by the feelings of sexual attraction, without the long-established "incest taboo" to control it. Persistent quarreling or hostilities between the young people sometimes signal their defense against these sexual stirrings. Sometimes the friendship between young people flowers into a deeper, sexual relationship. Parents can inadvertently intensify the problem by their early efforts to promote loving (platonic) relationships between the children in the interest of stepfamily harmony.

If parents and teens cooperate, sexual activity can be avoided. The trick, of course, is to get them to cooperate! Teens may resent having their freedom limited but should recognize that the situation requires appropriate and cautionary behavior, particularly with respect to a dress code in the home. Attractive sixteen-year-old Tamera reports:

> Before Mom and Erik got married, I used to walk between the bathroom and my bedroom in my underwear or a towel after a shower. I could sit in front of the TV or come to breakfast in my night clothes, or wear my bikini around the house in the summer time. Now that Erik's seventeen-year-old son Howard lives here, Mom says I have to wear a robe whenever I am not fully dressed. I understand why, but I forget sometimes, and I don't like having to remember.

To reduce the likelihood of stepteen sexual relationships developing, parents can:

♦ be aware of these possibilities and discuss sexual issues with their teens;

♦ discuss the facts of life with all pre-teen children as well as teens;

♦ avoid allowing too much unsupervised time to teens;

♦ avoid suppressing the natural tendency for teens to fight;

♦ encourage all children to talk about their sexual concerns and report any inappropriate behavior or touching;

♦ stress proper and modest dress except when in the privacy of their own rooms;

♦ encourage teens to develop outside friendships and activities.

If an attraction does develop between stepsiblings of the opposite sex, alternative living arrangements may assist the young people in managing the relationship during their school years until they are ready for other considerations.

Tim and Janese were young teen-agers when they became stepsiblings to each other. At first they did not like each other and not only fought frequently, but also traveled in different teen-age circles. As they matured during the next ten years, however, they fell in love. After college they were married in a lovely back yard wedding in their stepparents home.

Sexual attraction can also exist between stepparent and stepchild — the third sexual problem faced by some stepfamilies — because the natural biological bond and incest taboo prohibiting sexual activity between parents and children does not exist between stepchildren and stepparents. A stepfather may find in his attractive stepdaughter a younger version of his wife. An adolescent daughter, in her budding sexuality, may have a crush on her stepdad, but react with hostility out of confusion and guilt. Although sexual infatuations between stepmothers and stepsons occur less frequently, similar "crushes" do occasionally happen. Family therapists and steparents Ann Getzoff and Carolyn McClenahan address this concern in their book *Step Kids: A Survival Guide for Teenagers in Stepfamilies.* They remind stepfamilies to "recognize that these are normal feelings and are not dangerous in themselves, and, recognize and accept that you will never be able to act on those feelings."[4]

After family members get to know each other's human foibles and idiosyncracies and the stepfamily stabilizes, these feelings usually dissipate. Furthermore, Getzoff and McClenahan recommend that if either of the partners or a stepteen becomes aware of any sexual attraction problems, or someone's feelings of physical attraction become confused and unmanageable, a counselor specializing in stepfamily sexual issues should be consulted.

Having a Child in Common

A final important area of consideration for remarrying couples is the possibility of having a child together, either by birth into the family or adoption. Whether to have a child or not should be discussed prior to marriage, for men and women in remarriage often view the choice of adding a child to the family differently. Since husbands are usually older than their wives, and may already have children to support from a previous marriage, they frequently do not want more children, especially if there are stepchildren to support as well. Some women feel that the desire to have a child in common completes their relationship with their new husband. Other non-parent partners feel the biological clock ticking and desire a child as soon as possible.

Timing can be critical for the addition of a child to a stepfamily. Dr. Patricia Papernow, a psychologist specializing in stepfamilies in Newtownville, Massachusetts, is a stepparent and the mother of a toddler. In *Stepfamily Bulletin* she writes: "Whether the impact of a new child creates relief or a new source of tension seems strongly related to the stepfamily's stage of development."[5] Two important tasks stepfamilies face are coping with the differences between step and biological relationships, then building strong stepfamily bonds. Once the stepfamily stabilizes, a new child can be "a source of integration in a stepfamily, as everyone in the family finally has someone to whom all are biologically related."

In regard to adding new children, stepparents ask, "How will I feel toward my own child verses my stepchildren? How will the stepchildren accept our new baby?" Frequently, non-parent remarrieds are surprised at the intense emotional ties they feel for their first biological child, then feel guilty for not having the same attachment toward their stepchildren. It is usually impossible to feel that same intensity for stepchildren; however, both parents and stepchildren, with help, can adjust to the difference between stepparent love and parent love, as long as each person is reassured that he or she is loved and belongs to the family. Remarrieds who add children to their new family after the first stages of stepfamily bonding occur find that their existing children accept the new family member as long as they are reassured that the new child does not replace them in their parent's or stepparent's affections. In fact, with appropriate preparation, existing children enthusiastically look forward to the new family member and can be a real resource to the family and the new child in its formative years.

Stepfamily Living

Therapists say that any family functions best when the adult couple is the strongest unit and works as a team. Therefore, it is critical that the newly forming stepfamily recognize the reality of stepfamily living and begin to prepare for the task at hand. Dr. Patricia Papernow, in her two part series "The Stepfamily Cycle — Seven Steps to Familydom,"[6] states that the stepfamily task is to move from:

one mini-family with an outsider stepparent,

or

two mini-families living together in conflict,

to

a family unified by a strong cooperative couple.

Everyone must adjust and accommodate to other members of the family over time so that this task can be successfully completed.

Dr. Papernow identifies the early, middle, and late stages that stepfamilies experience as they work to become a successful stepfamily. In the early stage, the stepfamily is divided along biological lines, either one mini-family and a stepparent, or two mini-families. Everyone fantasizes about how the family will love and respect each other.

Frequently after a few months the family relationships are in chaos due to resistance to necessary change. For example, the family that always picks up after itself collides with the family that leaves things in disorder; the family that always eats dinner together faces the family that eats on the run; the family that schedules

TV time confronts the family that keeps TV on as background noise. Everyone feels frustrated, angry, guilty, and a sense of failure. Initially, the stepparent feels responsible for the failure. As time passes, however, he or she begins to see that it is not one-sided.

According to Dr. Papernow, nearly every stepparent can identify the incident that caused him or her to take a stand and stick to it. This ushers in the middle stage in which the family structures begin to unfreeze and shift. It is a period of conflict and competition for the affection of family members. It is also the period when the couple can "go into business together" in terms of managing this new family. Family members begin to listen to each other and solve problems creatively. Couples begin to work together to invent rules that balance the needs of all members of the family. Stepparent and stepchildren begin to work things out between them, and the stepparent moves into a disciplinary role.

In the late stage, the new stepfamily structure is in place and energy is now used to build closeness and a family history. By this time, individuals let go of things that cannot be changed. They become more accepting and settle into their new lifestyle. Basically, the stepfamily solidifies with reliable and nourishing relationships.

Dr. Papernow concludes that couples who are able to empathize, support, and understand the other person's position (children included) successfully negotiate these stages. Understanding the pain and frustration of the other and acknowledging out loud to each other the difficulty of becoming a stepfamily advances the movement toward reorganized successful stepfamily living. Time and care is needed to build these close family bonds. In her work, Dr. Papernow noted that fast families negotiated to successful stepfamily living in four years, the average family in seven years. Some families never do, and end up in a very dissatisfying family relationship or eventually divorce. The difference is determined by how long it takes the family members to negotiate through the early stages with empathy and support for each other.

New issues continue to arise in successful stepfamilies as in all families, but these issues can be handled when the following factors are present:

- there is a build-up of trust;
- family members listen and empathize with each other;

- the couple bond is strong (couple must spend alone time without kids regularly in order to develop that couple bond);
- the couple work as a strong team;
- there is a current history of resolving conflict;
- a family history has been established.

Most successful stepfamilies have a tremendous feeling of confidence and mastery, even years later. This sense of accomplishment enriches the happiness that these second married couples frequently speak about.

Conclusion

Although stepparenting is the most complicated dynamic of remarried living, and some marriages fail because of its stress, successful stepfamily living generates many rich, long-term benefits. For those who stick through the tough first months, it becomes a rich opportunity for personal growth and rewarding relationships. Successful remarrieds speak of the stepfamily as a creative learning center with great possibilities for all. Children have a variety of role models from which to gain new information and shared values. All family members:

- adjust to the reality that the world is not always just or fair;
- learn that flexibility and change are the key to survival and personal growth;
- grow by converting obstacles into steppingstones;
- discover the great nuances and joys of various kinds of love;
- respect individuals, regardless of age;
- become more sensitive to diverse views and accept new people;
- establish coping skills for working with others in relationship;
- develop lifelong, creative conflict resolution skills;
- commit themselves to working at love.

With an attitude of openness, patience, flexibility, prayer, and a willing spirit, a couple can facilitate growing relationships of respect, friendship, and love in the new family. Listed at the end of the chapter are some helpful hints to prepare you for stepfamily living.

Finally, realize you have support. Besides the assistance you may receive from a counselor, there is a wonderful supportive organization: The Stepfamily Association of America, Inc. It seeks to support stepfamilies' needs and concerns at all stages of development with resource people and materials, support groups, seminars and conferences, and an excellent quarterly, *Stepfamily Bulletin.* All are designed to assist stepfamilies with their unique problems and foster peaceful and successful stepfamily living. I strongly encourage you to call or write to the central office of SAA, listed in the resources at the back of the book, to find the contact person in your area who will connect you with the local resources available to you.

Helpful Hints

1. Be Prepared! You are creating a new family system in which everyone belongs. Old rules and expectations based on first marriage experience generally don't apply here.

2. Take time before marriage to "court" stepchildren with family activities, providing an opportunity to get to know each other and begin the bonding process.

3. Consider taking a few family counseling sessions and a re-marriage preparation course to prepare for merging your two families. Also, do some reading on good parenting skills and stepfamily living.

4. Have Patience! Move slowly, allow time to bond. A stepparent is a stranger in a child's life and the child needs to get to know and trust you.

5. Avoid interference with the children's access to their natural parents. Never criticize a child's parent in front of the child. It is critical to each child's well-being that he or she is free to love and be loved by them. Don't compete with the child's natural parents. Develop your own natural and unique relationship style with the children.

6. Strive toward an adult friendship with each stepchild. Don't expect more. Give sincere compliments or appreciations to each child daily.

7. In the beginning, let the natural parent take the lead in the discipline of his or her children. Settle differences in private but provide a united front as you support each other in front of the children. Whenever possible negotiate differences with children. Be fair and give due respect to all children.

8. Try a "family meeting." Get the children involved as much as reasonable and possible in setting family rules. Listen to become aware of the children's feelings and concerns. Help them experience the natural or logical consequences of their behavior, thus promoting responsible behavior and self-esteem.

9. Avoid discounting or criticizing your partner in front of others, especially children. Work out differences in private.

10. Spend individual time with each child in the family. Time with your own child reinforces and reaffirms his or her loving relationship with you. Time with each stepchild provides an opportunity to develop a trusting and caring bond.

11. Give regular quality private time to your couple relationship in order to form a solid couple bond.

12. Recognize and accept that creating a healthy, happy, and successful stepfamily takes preparation, patience, lots of love and acceptance, flexibility, prayer, and time — at least three to five years.

Stepparenting
WORKSHEET

Privately answer the questions, or respond to statements with *Agree* or *Disagree*. Then share with your partner.

1. I feel I am/will be a good parent/stepparent.

2. I am comfortable with my partner's children.

3. My expectations about being a stepparent or in a stepfamily are . . .

4. My children like/do not like my partner (circle one).

5. I expect my children to support our marriage.

6. With the exception of adding my partner to our family life, I do not expect any other significant changes in our family lifestyle.

7. We agree on what the role of parent/stepparent is in raising our children.

8. I am somewhat fearful of becoming a stepparent.

9. I worry that some of the children will cause friction between us.

10. There is no question in my mind that my partner will be a good parent/stepparent.

11. We have told our children of our intention to marry.

12. I agree with my partner's beliefs about disciplining children.

13. We have similar attitudes about what we want our children to get out of life.

14. I am not afraid to accept the responsibilities of being a parent/ stepparent.

15. Our styles of childraising are compatible.

16. I am concerned about how our children will get along with each other.

17. I am comfortable with allowing my partner some time alone with his/her children.

18. We are in agreement in our attitudes about birth control.

19. I want us to have a child together.

20. I will have physical custody of some/all/none of my children.

21. I am the non-custodial parent of some/all/none of my children.

22. How are child visitations occurring now? How will they continue or change after our marriage?

23. When my children come for their usual visit, they are my guests, and I want to do whatever they want to do.

24. When my children visit, they should be free of any household responsibilities while they are guests in our home.

25. I am uncomfortable with my partner's co-parenting visits/conversations with his/her former spouse.

26. I sometimes feel excluded or jealous of my partner's relationship with his/her children.

27. My children's special needs are . . . (list according to each child).

28. My children's interests and activities are . . . (sports, music, art, science, etc.).

29. My children's special problems are . . .

30. When my children are sick, I usually . . .

31. Discipline is a problem with one or more of my children.

32. One thing I do not like about one or more of my partner's children is . . .

33. I want sole authority over the discipline of my children.

34. I want my partner to share in the discipline of my children in the following ways...

35. I expect to share in the discipline of my partner's children.

36. I believe in spanking or physical punishment for children who misbehave.

37. I believe one should never use physical punishment with children.

38. A child's behavior that I find absolutely unacceptable is...

39. I believe children should behave respectfully to all adults at all times.

40. I want my children to have reasonable freedom of expression in situations which involve them.

41. I believe our children's needs should always come before our own.

42. I sometimes resent the way my partner's children treat me/my partner.

43. Children should have responsibilities in the home (clean rooms, dishes, etc.).

44. Children should get an allowance for good grades or completing household chores.

45. Children should get an allowance without having worked for it.

46. Children should not get an allowance.

47. I prefer the family meeting form of governing the family.

48. What kind of family rules do I want our children to respect?

49. Only parents should determine family rules.

50. I want help and suggestions on how to raise my children to be responsible adults.

51. I expect children to be on their own and supporting themselves by the age of _____.

52. Working adult children living at home should contribute financially to the family.

53. I want our children to go to church with us and attend religious instruction.

54. We should never argue in front of the children.

55. I expect my partner to back me at all times in front of the children.

56. I expect to back my partner at all times in front of the children.

57. I believe we should always present a united front to our children regarding our decisions.

58. What kind of accommodations and sleeping arrangements do I want my children to have?

59. I am prepared to make permanent space available for visiting children.

60. With the exception of adding my partner to our family life, I expect there will not be any significant changes in my family's lifestyle.

61. What am I willing to do to help create this new family?

62. We need to plan for this new family to include all our needs, children and adults.

63. I want my older children to like my new partner.

64. I think we should get family counseling before we bring our families together.

65. I expect some problems with my former spouse regarding our children and their new stepparent.

66. Some possible conflicts we might have with my former spouse, or my partner's former spouse are . . .

67. I think my former spouse or my partner's former spouse will try to sabotage our relationship through the children.

68. My former spouse and I have ended our divorce war, particularly in regard to the children.

69. I do not want my partner to belittle or undermine me in front of the children.

70. I don't want to have anything to do with my partner's adult children.

71. What my adult children think of my new partner does not really matter to me.

72. I want to be called mom/dad by my stepchildren.

73. I want to adopt my stepchildren.

74. After a few months of adjustment, I believe our stepfamily will have very few problems.

75. My partner's parents and family accept me warmly.

76. I feel uncomfortable with my partner's parents and family.

77. Some members of my family resent my remarriage.

78. I am still close with my former in-laws and want to remain so.

79. I want my children to continue to see their grandparents.

80. I don't want to be in contact with my partner's former spouse.

81. I am willing, if necessary, to work with my partner's former spouse for the benefit of my stepchildren.

Additional Comments:

Safe Place

In a safe place, people are kind. Sarcasm, fighting, back-biting and name calling are exceptions. Kindness, consideration and forgiveness are the usual way of life.

In a safe place there is laughter; not just the canned laughter of TV but real laughter that comes from sharing meaningful work and play.

In a safe place there are rules. These rules are few and fair and are made by the people who live and work there, including the children.

In a safe place people listen to one another. They care about one another and show that they do.[7]

Mary MacCracken
Turnabout Children

Is your family a safe place for everyone?

CHAPTER 4

Finances, Houses,
Roles, Step Pets

---

*L*et not debt remain outstanding, except the continuing
debt to love one another.

— *Romans 13:8*

In our American culture today, money is a major concern. Those
who have it worry about losing it, those who don't have it worry
about getting it, and nearly everyone wants more! Let's look at our
financial values while we reflect and respond to these questions:

♦ What does money mean to you?

♦ How do you use or spend it?

♦ How does it meet your emotional and physical needs?

Do any of the responses below ring true for you?

"I am very insecure when money is tight. I am afraid I
won't be able to pay bills or even survive."
— *Bob, 45, consultant, remarried*

"I save for major items before I buy."
— *Carol, 56, nurse, remarried*

"I often buy on impulse and worry about paying later."
— *Mark, 32, lab technician, single*

"Money is a pick-up for me. When I get depressed I usually
go out and spend money on myself."
— *Walter, 33, salesman, married*

"Money is not important. If you are alive and healthy, you
can always make more money."
— *Rien, 70, engineer, married*

"For me, having plenty of money means freedom from financial worry."

— *Gary, 40, attorney, married*

"Money is the means to what I want."

— *Melissa, 29, secretary, single*

"Money means economic security, in that I have enough to take care of myself."

— *Joan, 35, teacher, divorced*

Money has more than a dollars and cents value for each of us. Emotional matters of power, self-esteem, fear, independence, anxiety, status, and commitment underlie most of our responses to financial concerns. Your thoughtful responses to the above questions may help you discover your emotionally laden feelings about money matters and which money values and expectations influence your lifestyle.

Barry Kaufman, in his book *To Love Is to Be Happy With,* writes about our emotional attachment to money:

> Some of us believe money is a sign of dignity and self-worth. Others envision it as man's corrupter, cementing him to materialistic garbage. Some want money to buy food and shelter. Others want it to buy love, happiness and immortality. Money, like love, health, or sex, is a multifaceted symbol to which we attach many fears and judgments. What we feel about money, how we gather it, has little to do with an intrinsic characteristic of currency . . . but everything to do with our beliefs and wants.[1]

In almost all marriages, financial issues trigger at least one major conflict. In second and subsequent marriages, these conflicts take on additional emotional facets because of past marital histories and stepfamily formation. Furthermore, couples in second marriages are more likely to have increased assets or own more personal property than first-married couples. Therefore, as we prepare to remarry, we must dare to discuss our money values and financial history, our money goals and expectations, and our personal assets and liabilities in order to reduce the likelihood of future financial pitfalls.

Financial History

Our financial values, like all our other values, form in our early life. What our parents said — and didn't say — about money and spending priorities influence our attitude toward money. Karen, a divorced woman of forty, outlines her money history:

> Money was always "hush-hush" in our family. I can still hear my dad's "It's none of your business" or mom's "We can't afford it" or "Don't discuss our personal business outside of our family." We learned early the unwritten rule: never ask questions about financial matters.
>
> Yet, as an average family, we had most of what we needed, and some of what we wanted. Dad was the primary breadwinner, and occasionally mom worked during a financial crunch. As a teen-ager, I babysat for personal money. I remember how excited and grown-up I felt the first Christmas I bought gifts for everyone from my own earned income. In my late teens I worked part-time.
>
> When I married soon after high school, I did not expect to work again, for my perceived role as wife and mother was to maintain a household and raise a family. During the next fifteen years my husband's income supported our family. In the three years prior to an unexpected divorce, I worked part-time to pay some bills and redecorate our home.
>
> When our marriage fell apart, I panicked. I worried about my financial survival; yet, I struggled to educate myself for the job market. Within four years, my financial status stabilized and I felt economically secure.

In the past, first-married couples usually lived on the income of one of the partners, or, if both persons worked, they most likely pooled their financial resources into a common fund from which all expenses were paid. Over the years the community property — mortgages, furniture, cars, stocks, bank accounts, pension funds — accumulated. Today, with the skyrocketing cost of living and housing, the changing roles of women, and the greater desire for and access to material possessions, both partners in a first marriage frequently work.

All assets are necessarily reorganized, sometimes depleted or divided, with a divorce. Singles painfully adjust to their new status. They set new goals, often re-establishing financial security through additional education and new working environments. Personal assets and liabilities frequently include spousal and/or child support income or payments, which divorced persons bring to the financial considerations of second marriage. Moreover, they quickly recognize that it will take two incomes to support the new family. When couples enter a second marriage, especially if there are children, a financial crisis again occurs, as all assets and liabilities must be evaluated and reorganized once more.

Few families or individuals perceive that they earn enough money to satisfy their needs and wants. Everyone also has their splurges and thrifty moments. Consequently, engaged persons should share their financial history and dream together so they can understand each other's personal view regarding finances, and better organize their monetary needs and desires in this new family.

Couples begin by telling each other how they feel about money, and the source of their perspective (i.e., family habits, ethnic or cultural background). For some, money is tied to their identity, and they jealously guard their money and possessions. Some generously share what they have through charities or churches, while others give sparingly of their extra funds only after their own needs and wants are met. One partner spends money freely to achieve social status, while the other desires to save money for retirement. One individual pays cash, while the other prefers credit. Some people favor saving money for a specific item such as a luxury car or boat, while others choose to save for "rainy day" emergencies. One views the savings as a vacation, while the other views it as a new addition to the house or inheritance for family members. Some consistently spend beyond their means or are impulse buyers, not saving a penny. They frequently find themselves coping with financial emergencies. Others, consumed by their quest for money, become miserly, collecting the almighty dollar and avoiding even necessary spending.

Many people in our culture today see money as the means to happiness. To minimize major clashes in money values, couples need to discuss how they spend money and their financial goals and expectations; then they can develop a financial plan that blends their needs, desires, and financial styles.

Merging Your Finances

Engaged couples must trust each other enough to disclose their assets and liabilities so they can assess their financial status and determine what money they want to merge and what, if any, they want to keep separate. Successful couples tailor a financial plan, using good budgeting skills, to accommodate their particular needs. Occasionally, capable partners take turns — on a monthly or yearly basis — maintaining the household budget. This allows each person the experience of carrying out the financial responsibilities of the family, as well as some freedom from the emotional stress of paying bills and handling financial emergencies.

Whenever possible, individuals should pay off their personal debts and credit cards before the wedding. If a financial obligation is too large to complete before the marriage, an individual may personally maintain the obligation out of his or her own earnings after marriage. Sometimes, couples decide to pool income and expenses, as in first marriages. Other two-income couples contribute an equal percentage of individual income into a joint account for general household and living expenses such as rent or mortgage, food, utilities, and charitable contributions. They may also equally contribute to a joint savings account for a specific use such as a vacation, emergencies, or retirement. One couple from our workshops indicated that they save for an additional "fun fund" to which each adds loose change and small bills. After general contributions to joint accounts, individuals retain any leftover money for personal use.

The flexibility with which couples allocate their incomes depends on the amount of income, their financial responsibilities, and their ability to successfully manage their finances. Furthermore, those who contribute to the family income in the spirit of sharing and generosity, rather than with a nit-picking approach, circumvent much financial tension.

Separate Money

Individuals who have lived as single, autonomous adults for even a few years are reluctant to give up all financial independence in marriage. This is especially true for those who struggled to gain financial security after the emotional and financial devastation of divorce. They fear a second financial crisis. Both men and women in marriage want to share with their spouse financial decisions regarding the family income disbursement, but they also want some money of their own to spend or save as they wish.

Joyce and Victor told us their story of a difficult money situation they faced after they married:

"I could not disclose my money problems and high debts to Joyce while we were engaged," explained Victor. "I was afraid she would not marry me if she knew that I owed several thousand dollars. After we married, she found out anyway, when the collection agencies came calling."

"I was very upset," said Joyce. "If we could have discussed it in advance we could have determined how to handle the situation. We did manage to pay the money back with the aid of some of my savings. At first I was very angry, not because of the money, but because of his lack of trust in me."

In a recent panel discussion on two-income couples, California attorney Nancy Rodriquez questioned the panel on personal spending: "How much money should your partner spend without consulting you?" and the reverse, "How much do you think you should be able to spend without consulting your partner?" There was general agreement that this would exclude food and clothes. The answers ranged from $25 to $1,000 depending on the couple's income. Nancy comments on the discussion:

> What I find fascinating is the underlying money values that emerged in the discussion of the question. One doctor in a high income bracket indicated that he isn't as concerned about the amount as how it is spent. He stated, "I wouldn't want my wife to independently purchase a vacation trip for us to someplace in Europe without consulting me." Another participant clarified his position in that consulting one's partner is not asking for permission. Some persons expressed concern about spending beyond their income. Others commented that the amount isn't as important as the consultative value to the marriage of sharing ideas, choices and participation in major purchases. In addition, most participants agreed that each person should have some personal money to spend as they choose.

Ask yourself the same questions and explain why you chose a particular amount and what items you might include or not include in your spending. Furthermore, design a method by which each of you can have some personal spending money, no matter how small the amount.

Support Money

Handling support monies, a highly emotional issue, complicates second marriages enormously. There are two aspects to this problem that remarrieds must face: support money income and support money expense.

Support Income:　When children and stepchildren live within the family unit, couples must decide whether to combine all support income or set it into separate accounts for specific children. Next, they must determine how to allocate the funds for children's expenses. Some couples, whose joint incomes barely cover the needs of the family, do not have much flexibility in their financial distributions. Therefore, they choose to combine all money and distribute it equally among the children's needs. When parents separate the money of individual children into separate accounts, jealousy and competition sometimes develop between children, especially when some children have more funds for clothes or special activities than others. Regardless of the amount for each child, perceptive parents distribute the funds for needs and activities fairly to avoid competition that may permanently disrupt the family unit.

Reverend Neal A. Kuyper, in his article "When Eight Is Enough," shares the creative and workable solution to cope with fair distribution of funds that he and his wife, Christine, settled upon. They formed a family of eight when he combined his four adolescents with Christine's two adolescents. The financial structure that they established follows:

> We adjusted the allowances to [our children's] ages. We made a list of household chores. . . . Each had to give their room a good cleaning once a week. Mother would do the laundry, but each child would do his/her own ironing. We set a limit on what we would pay toward clothing. If they wanted a more expensive store, they could pay the extra. . . . Each paid five cents a mile for the use of the car. . . . We determined the basic amount we could contribute toward college educations. The children would have to earn the rest or obtain student loans. . . . We established a set amount of money we could spend for each birthday, graduation, and Christmas . . . weddings . . . grandchildren.[2]

Frequently support income arrives late or not at all. Because most stepfamily income is stretched to the limit, this stresses the couple relationship emotionally as well as financially. Many stepfathers feel angry at assuming total support of the stepchildren when the absent parent refuses to pay his share of the responsibility. The mother of these children also expresses anger, sometimes by withholding visitation rights from the absent, non-paying parent.

Support Expenses. When a significant share of the family income leaves the family household to support a former spouse or children, it creates the second sensitive money issue for remarrieds. Although these important obligations must be met, they contribute to the money squeeze that many remarried couples face. The stepfather may feel guilty because he must contribute close to half of his income to the outside support of a former wife and/or children from his first marriage, while his present spouse's income is the primary support of the new family. Second wives often resent this income imbalance. A woman may work to support the family, while half of her new husband's earnings is earmarked for first marriage financial obligations.

For example, Nancy, as a college professor, earns a smaller salary than her second husband, Clarke, a marketing manager for a large company. However, half of his income is paid out in spousal and child support, while Nancy's income carries the major load of the family expenses. She also receives child support for her two boys, but it is considerably less than Clarke's support for his children. Moreover, Nancy's child support frequently comes late or never arrives. Consequently, both Clarke and Nancy feel disturbing emotions of guilt and resentment, which seriously stress the relationship.

Two other typical situations are listed below.

"While we were dating," says Marsha, remarried for two years with the custody of her elementary school children, "Joe and I seemed to have enough money to spend on some extras — small trips, clothes, dinner out. When we remarried, I lost spousal support and gained the additional expense of helping to save money to bring Joe's kids out here during the summer. I feel frustrated and angry with the money situation, as we rarely have money for extras. Sometimes Joe takes the brunt of my frustration. Life for us was so much easier before we were married."

"Jack pays his former wife $800 per month for her and his two children," says JoAnn. "When Jack's kids come to visit, they show up in their worst clothes — grubby jeans, and tee shirts. I am ashamed to take them anywhere. When we buy them extra clothes and they take them home, we never see the clothes again. Even on our wedding day, Jack had to make an emergency trip to the store for some dress clothes because the children arrived in their jeans, although their mother knew they were coming to the wedding. We've started to maintain a small wardrobe for them here so they will have a change of clothes and we don't have to purchase new clothes each time they visit."

Sometimes, the income of one or both partners in the second marriage increases. This may signal a former spouse to ask for more support money, which causes another upheaval in the financial and emotional climate of the second marriage.

Each couple must discuss this complex issue of support-money management before marriage, not only to express their financial concerns, needs, and desires but also to listen to the deep feelings and concerns of the other with a loving and understanding heart. They also must look at future possibilities realistically and make some contingency plans. With the assistance of a counselor and an attorney, they can sort out their financial obligations, their assets, and their specific support issues, and then tailor a flexible financial plan to suit their particular incomes and marital situation, accommodating fairly their obligations to past marriages and their new family's needs and responsibilities.

Legal Assistance

I recommend that every engaged couple consult an attorney who specializes in family law and estate planning at least three to six months prior to the wedding or within one or two months after the decision to marry. Major areas that engaged couples should discuss with an attorney are:

1. Review of past Marriage Settlement Agreements (MSA):

- ♦ clarify ongoing financial obligations from first marriages, especially support obligations;

- ♦ complete any unfinished business from the settlement that may affect the new marriage, such as beneficiaries to

insurance or pension plans, and claims on the estate of the
present individual by the first spouse or children;

♦ review any transfer of assets or titles from former marriage.

Sometimes couples forget to clear up details from their divorce
settlements that could impinge on the rights of the second spouse,
as in John and Carole's situation.

When Carole and John were divorced two years ago, their
1981 Ford was declared Carole's property in the Marital
Settlement Agreement. However, neither Carole nor John
transferred ownership at the DMV. When Carole was in
a recent accident, the owner of the other car decided to
sue. As a result, both John and Carole were named in
the lawsuit. Although the MSA established clearly that
John was not responsible for the car, John had to retain
an attorney at some cost of time and money to file the
appropriate papers clearing his name from the legal action.

2. Explore Pre-Marital Agreements (PMA):

♦ review problems and possibilities regarding separate property
versus community property;

♦ understand the legal impact of co-mingling property;

♦ review tax implications, insurance protection, investments,
pensions for new marriage;

♦ make financial arrangements relating to inheritances or possible future income; explore protection of the new spouse
in case of changes in support agreements or death of the
partner;

♦ check protection for the financial, educational, and guard-
ianship of young children in case of the untimely death of
the parent.

A Pre-Marital Agreement (sometimes called a Pre-Nuptial
Agreement or Contract) is a legal document designed by the couple
with the professional assistance of an attorney. Signed just before
the marriage, the PMA usually defines which property they wish
to keep separate and which they intend to become community
property. PMAs are not set in concrete. They may be altered at

any time according to the marital status and the changing needs of the new family.

Tim and Laura, each previously divorced, have remarried. Tim has a financial note from his former wife on the house they owned together in which his former wife still lives. In Laura and Tim's PMA, they designated that when the first house is sold, his share of the money will remain his separate property. Laura designated an inheritance account from her parents as her separate property. Tim and Laura also defined their incomes as separate, but they each con-tribute a portion of their income into a common fund from which they take care of the household expenses. Any prop-erty they accumulate after marriage becomes community property.

At the time of their marriage, they each contributed an agreed upon amount of dollars toward the purchase of their new home. If the house is sold or there is an unexpected death or divorce, the spouse(s) will reimburse themselves their original contribution, then split the re-maining equity.

Since Tim pays child support, he set up a special insurance policy to cover any remaining child support if he dies before his children are twenty years old. This policy protects Laura from having to pay his child support from his estate.

Not everyone wants or needs a premarital agreement. It de-pends on whether each person has substantial assets or large per-sonal debts and or responsibilities remaining from the first marriage or single life. However, exploring the possibility of a PMA is well worth the time and energy, and may save some future financial anguish.

In our workshops, couples sometimes express concern that drawing up a PMA implies distrust of one another or contemplation of future divorce. Laura responds to this:

We found it risky, awkward and stressful at first to talk about our personal money matters. However, both Tim and I believe in our commitment of love to each other, so we took the risk. We both feel that our honesty with each other on these tough issues draws us closer rather than hurting our relationship. We trust and respect each other more because we have revealed our deepest feelings and concerns about losing what we gained as singles. We see the PMA as a public statement and commitment to our financial trust in each other, an acknowledgment of the reality that there are no guarantees for the future, regardless of our best intentions, and the way we can properly tend to the responsibilities from previous marriages. Furthermore, our PMA and our wills provide the best protection and possibilities for the children should one or both of us die. As our life together evolves and our children reach adulthood, we intend to modify our agreement and our wills so they always reflect our current status and meet the changing needs of our family.

3. Prepare new wills:

♦ review any pre-existing wills; explore how you want your estates distributed at your death;

♦ draw up new wills;

♦ check for consistency between your PMA (if you have one) and your wills, your beneficiaries, insurance policies, trusts, pension plans, and any other important documents.

Without a will, the state determines your executor, appoints a guardian for any minor children, and distributes your estate according to the dictates of the law. Your written will puts you, not the state, in control of the distribution of your hard-earned assets and prized possessions.

Also, some wills written before marriage (depending on the state law) are revoked in favor of a statutory claim of a new spouse on the estate of his or her partner unless specifically stated otherwise in a codicil to the old will or in a new will. In addition, a pre-existing will — not updated after a second marriage — can present a problem for a surviving second spouse. Attorney Nancy Rodriguez explains:

Mary drew up a will after her divorce, leaving her house to her three adult children at her death. Two years later, Mary married John, however she neglected to update her will. When she was killed suddenly in an automobile accident and the estate was settled, the adult children, claiming their estate, asked John to leave the house. If Mary had updated her will at the time of her second marriage, she could have left the house to her children, but included a life-estate clause which would allow John to live in the house for a specific period of time, until he chooses to leave, or until his own death occurs.

The discussion between marital partners of "last things" can be fearful and stressful at first. However, such discussions and decisions based on careful planning and mature judgments, are an act of kindness for all concerned, because it reduces the legal financial burden and the possibility of problems for the survivors in the midst of grieving their loss. Those couples who provide for the distribution of their assets and their prized possessions, who choose the significant people to administer their estate, and who provide for the needs and care of their survivors through a written will, claim that they feel reassured and more peaceful at having made these difficult decisions.

Finding an Attorney

The professional assistance of a competent, ethical attorney can be invaluable when managing the complicated financial issues resulting from remarriage. Seeking legal counsel requires some time and money; it is an investment in the arrangement of your financial future.

Attorneys, like other professionals, specialize. Many are state certified in their specialties. Check with your friends, family, and associates for recommendations of attorneys who specialize in family law and/or estate planning. If unsuccessful, call the local lawyer referral service or bar association for recommendations. Remember, you hire an attorney to work for you, to advise you of your rights and the laws regarding your situation, and make recommendations for your consideration. You, however, make the decisions based on his or her expertise and your needs.

Many attorneys offer an initial one hour consultation appointment at a special reduced rate. Be prepared to pay the consultation fee on the day of your appointment, as attorneys usually do not bill this type of fee. Couples frequently interview two or three attorneys before selecting the one whom they feel will best represent them. By phone call, ask the attorney about his or her qualifications and experience in your particular legal matter, his or her success record in such matters, the consultation fee, and the hourly rate; then set an appointment. Prepare for your office visit.

1. Outline or summarize your situation on paper before the appointment to be clear in your mind as to your needs and your questions.

2. Bring your notes with you, and any documents to support your situation (i.e., MSA, divorce papers, insurance policies, wills).

3. During the appointment, confirm the attorney's recent experience in this specialty and the consultation fee. Then briefly summarize your situation and ask pertinent questions. Listen to the attorney and, if you wish, write down the responses.

4. Before the end of your appointment, ask how the attorney will bill the time (hourly rate or flat fee) should you retain him or her. Ask about retainers (an initial deposit), fee agreements, itemized monthly billings, and the anticipated cost of handling the matter for you. Furthermore, ask what the attorney will need from you if you retain him or her.

5. Pay your consultation fee to the attorney or office secretary before you leave.

6. After you have consulted two or three attorneys, retain the one whom you believe will best work with you and for you.

Please note: Each of the states in the United States may have similar but technically different laws regarding these matters. For instance, not all states are community property states, and the laws regarding community property will greatly affect your PMA and your estate matters. Therefore, consulting an attorney may clear away any confusion as you prepare to make these important decisions.

Whose House?

"Where are we going to live, your place or mine, or should we buy a new house?" Most counselors suggest that whenever possible, the couple choose a new home of their own — neutral territory — to begin their life together. To remain in one or the other's place, especially if the home was occupied by the present partner and former spouse, frequently disturbs the new marriage. As the incoming partner confronts the ghosts of the past partner, this new spouse often feels like he or she is invading the other's previous marital territory, or feels like a guest in the other's home. Memories, expectations, and hidden competition with the past relationship, stimulated by the familiar surroundings, stirs beneath the surface and may break down the foundation of the new marriage.

If a couple begins their marriage in a place of their own choosing, they stand equal as they enter this new stage of their relationship. In making such a decision, of course, complications arise. If each partner owns a home, those homes must be rented or sold. When one or both of the partners holds title to a house with a former spouse, they may be limited on changes they can make. In some instances, new spouses buy out the former spouse's interest in the home.

In the event that the engaged couple cannot or chooses not to move into a new residence, they ease the transition into one or the other's home by making some changes reflecting their changing marital status. Frequently couples redecorate by painting, choosing some new furnishings and accessories, and rearranging the furniture. Other couples build an addition on to the house to accommodate their new status and needs. All changes should reflect shared decision-making. No matter what changes occur, it behooves the welcoming partner to make every effort to provide psychological and physical space for his or her mate, taking in consideration the other's needs and interests. Couples say it takes many months, even years, of adjustment for the incoming partner to feel at home.

Larry, my husband, describes his experience of moving in and adjusting to my house:

> Bobbi and I, for economic reasons, chose to live in her home from her previous marriage. To prepare for the change, we bought new carpet, some new furniture — including a new bed — changed small accessories to accommodate my interest in sailing, and set up an extra bedroom as an office for us both. Bobbi cleaned out closets and drawers to make space for me before I arrived. We discussed our likes and dislikes about decorating and furniture styles and discovered some differences, which we worked through.

We both love books and we found a way to include all our books. I have also put my mark on this house by building some cabinets, changing one room into a dining room, and making other small carpentry changes. It took me some time to learn the established system of the household, especially the kitchen. For instance, I enjoy cooking and through trial and error, I learned how the kitchen was organized, where to find utensils and dishes. Even with all her effort made to welcome me, it took about two years before I could comfortably say "our home."

Natale discovered some strong disturbing feelings after moving into Joe's house:

When I married Joe, a single, never-married person, we sold my house from my former marriage, stored or sold most of my furniture, and moved into Joe's home. Within two months, I felt dissatisfied with the fact that nothing in the house was mine or reflected my style and tastes. I spoke to a friend about my increasing discomfort; she suggested that we purchase a new bed together (his bed was small and not very comfortable). After discussing it with Joe, we purchased new bedroom furniture, leading to other mutual purchases, which alleviated much of my stress. Four years later, we sold that house and bought a new one. Now I feel on a equal basis and our home is *our* home.

Territory

Along with a house comes the difficult decision of determining which furniture, household items, and decorations to keep and which to dispose of. Some couples review their duplicates, keep the best, and give the rest to charity. Others may pass on the leftover household goods to their adult children or have a garage sale to earn extra funds to purchase new items.

When my children left home to set up housekeeping in their first apartment, before I met Larry, they cleaned me out of duplicate household items. Any extra kitchen utensils, bedding or other linens, plus their own bedroom furniture, went with them. Anything that they thought they could use, and I did not need, they took. It is very expensive to set up housekeeping these days without some of mother's donations! A remarrying couple could do the same for any children soon to leave home. If children are still young, a box of goods could be prepared for them from some of the leftovers of your two households. (Remember the old-fashioned "hope chest" of a generation or two ago?)

One of the items Larry brought to our marriage was a set of brand new, deep purple towels that he and his first wife had received as a wedding gift. They did not use them during their marriage for the same reason I did not want to use them: the color was inappropriate for our home. We kept them packed away for a year until Larry decided that we should give them to a charitable organization.

Every individual accumulates items of sentimental value over the years — picture albums, a favorite rocking chair, a figurine, trophies, a wall hanging. These treasures are not easily discarded, for they not only have great personal value but also represent territory and identity for each individual, especially as he or she moves into someone else's home. Wherever the couple resides, each spouse must be allowed to bring these special personal belongings or household items into the home. Usually a place can be found for such treasures. Larry speaks of it as a territorial need:

> One of the items I brought to our marriage was a fern, an off-shoot from the drain hole of a plant that my first wife and I had. When we parted, she took the big plant, I took the seedling, nursing it into a small, thriving plant. In two years, in Bobbi's living room it flourished, outgrowing the pot. One day I found Bobbi carefully breaking it apart and replanting the new shoots. Although I felt very angry that she hadn't asked my permission to re-pot it, I said nothing. A few years later in one of our classes, I used that incident as an illustration of the meaning of owning territory in someone else's home. Of course she was surprised and apologetic about that incident, and wished that I had called her attention to it at the time. Three lessons were learned from that experience: 1) territory often is represented by small, seemingly insignificant, items; 2) respecting individual territory is very important; 3) harboring hurts or anger blocks the relationship.

Another couple, Ed and Mary Jane, handled their territorial

situation very creatively, and at the same time enhanced their relationship and their home.

> "When Ed and I married," stated Mary Jane, "we agreed that he would sell his own home and buy out my former husband's interest in my house. When he moved in, he brought his scraggly, old, very comfortable, favorite chair. We both agreed that it would not be an appropriate piece of furniture for the living room, yet I knew Ed loved it and did not want to part with it. Since I had an extra room, we decided to make a den for Ed in which he could keep his books, computer, drawing board, and his favorite chair. When we finished, the problem was solved, resulting in a satisfying accommodation of both our needs."

During adult life our individual tastes in art, music, style, and design often evolve into very strong likes and dislikes. If we have been married before, our preferences evolved with another person. When we marry again, we can be surprised that our preferences clash with those of our new spouse. Some of this conflict may also result from our desire to maintain our individuality as well as our territorial needs as we merge our life with another. These conflicts frequently lead to new growth in intimacy and understanding if we explore our tastes and preferences, and reinforce the areas on which we agree, rather than emphasize our differences. Later, when we shop, we are more likely to find new acceptable styles that reflect both of our preferences and needs.

Roles and Household Tasks

Only occasionally did Leon or I, as singles living alone, prepare large meals at specific times or maintain our homes in specific ways. Except for our jobs, we were free to go and do as we chose without many time constraints or consideration of others. When we prepared to marry, we both recognized that our lives would change, in that we would have to consider and consult each other. Contrary to my first marriage of twenty years, I wasn't interested in being the chief cook and bottle washer or doing all the housework, washing, and cleaning. Leon wasn't either, so we planned the management of our household, sharing responsibilities so both of us had some free time. Leon, a good cook, and I prepare meals and do the clean-up together. It's the time when we share our day's experiences. Whoever notices that laundry needs to be done starts the washer. Each of us uses the sewing machine and the iron as needed. Whenever we expect company, we work together to prepare for our guests. When one of us is tired, the other takes over. Sometimes we take turns doing whatever needs to be done.

Couples frequently discover that their roles in this new marriage differ from those of their first marriage and that of the single life, as Carol emphasized in the preceding example. Engaged couples need to discuss their expectations of married life and their roles in the family, particularly if both are working. If their family life will include children living at home, all family members can rotate responsibilities on a weekly or monthly basis. Use of family meetings and shared decision-making offers newly forming families an alternative approach to regulating household routines and activities. Above all, a cooperative and flexible spirit between partners and family members promotes the smooth operation of a harmonious household.

One of the surprises in my marriage to Larry occurred when I realized how deeply my own programing about being a wife and mother was ingrained. I viewed myself as totally responsible for the maintenance of the household. I could accept some occasional assistance, but unrealistic guilt reared its ugly head when Larry did the washing or even ironed his own shirt. I could not sit and read the paper while he prepared the evening meal, even though he loves to cook. Fortunately, Larry does not have the same expectation of me, for he was third in a family of eleven children and participated in household routines for many years.

I have loosened guilt's grip on me, however, by taking a good rational look at those instilled values in the light of my present experience. Larry and I both work outside the home five days a week, plus we are busy on some evenings and many weekends. We have some spare time in which to maintain relationships with our families and do some extra things for ourselves. Because we value our time together, we share household responsibilities. Larry affirms my effort to loosen the bonds of the previous values that no longer apply to us today. Now, when inappropriate guilt nudges me, I happily ignore it!

Step Pets

Animals are important and loved members of many households. Often, Fido or Fluffy grew up as companions to the children. Dissension arises when the new partner objects to animals or reacts allergically to them. Confusion and chaos also occur in a household when each spouse has animals and the animals don't get along.

In one remarrying family, the husband had a large boxer, the wife had a toy poodle; she had a garden-variety cat, he had a pair of Siamese cats. After bringing the animals together, one of his cats ran away, causing him much unhappiness and the remaining Siamese some trauma. The other animals eventually tolerated each other, although initially the couple questioned whether the two dogs would ever get along. Another couple mentioned in one of our classes that whenever they cuddled up on the couch, her small dog would jump between them, growling.

Bob and Kerry told us their step pet story.

"One evening shortly after we were married, we arrived home to discover that my bird cage was empty," states Bob. "We followed the trail of feathers and found, much to my dismay, that Kerry's purring Siamese cat had eaten my $80 canary! Since then the cat has been living her ninth life as an outdoor cat."

The funniest story I have heard came from John, one of our *Once More With Love* participants:

One evening, shortly after Lulu and I met, I stopped by to pick her up for a dinner date. Lulu's large, friendly dog accompanied the two of us on a quick tour of her home. While passing through Lulu's bedroom, she left to answer the phone. Caesar (the dog) immediately lifted his leg on the upholstered chair near me. About that time Lulu returned. She was shocked by Caesar's surprising behavior. Lulu said he had not done that since he was a pup. I laughingly commented that Caesar appeared to be stating his territorial boundaries, and was challenging me to do the same!

Ann Genett, in *Stepfamily Bulletin*, Fall 1985, shares her story of her beloved fox terrier, Ziggy, who became quite ill shortly after her second husband moved into her condo. After a series of expensive tests, the veterinarian concluded that Ziggy was re-acting to the stress of a new person's presence in the home. The veterinarian prescribed the treatment of time to get used to each other and a daily dose of Maalox to sooth Ziggy's nervous stomach. Today, Ziggy is a happy, healthy, friendly dog who loves his new family, and prefers Maalox to a Milk-Bone!

Two examples show how creativity, humor, and fate can solve the dog-days of coping with pets in second marriages:

> Until I married Keith, I had never owned any pets. Keith, however, had two dogs that were his former wife's pets. When she left their marriage, she left her dogs as well. I don't mind dogs, but when I married Keith, although the dogs were never hostile toward me, they vomited every time they came in the house when I was there. It happened so frequently that I concluded that they did not like me. Keith resisted the idea until he witnessed their behavior a few times. The dogs died within the year, most likely grieving the loss of Keith's first wife.

> Martha and Jim each have animals from their former, single lives. Jim's dog chases cats. Martha owns a parrot and a cat, who often covets the bird as a mealtime treat! Rather than get rid of their beloved pets, they arranged for the cat to reside in the basement, the bird in the cage, and the dog outside. However, each day, each of the animals are allowed time for a free run of the house. Both Jim and Martha organize those occasions so only one animal is loose at a time. They have managed this menagerie successfully, with only one or two near misses, for five years.

Elder Care

One other area that occasionally emerges in our classes is coping with the care of aging and ailing parents. America is aging. In the 1980s, child care was a major concern for working parents. Elder care has become a growing concern of the 1990s. We see and hear about it on television and radio, in the papers and magazines. It is a hot issue in Congress and many families face it in their homes. The fastest growing segment of the population in the United States is the over–85 group. Because of the rapid development in medical cures and care, we live longer. Living longer means years of fruitful and happy living for many elders and chronic ill health or dying in small increments of disease for others.

Some remarrying couples become members of the "sandwich generation" — those people who are parenting their frail or ill parents or relatives while still caring for their own children. Sometimes a household includes a live-in independent parent, which will certainly impact the new marriage. Other times, the possibility of an aging relative residing in the home appears imminent, especially if he or she is in poor health. In addition, aging relatives may become suddenly ill, as in the case of stroke or heart attack, and require immediate attention of family members. The loving, respectful, and constant care of a frail person frequently produces stress, and coping mechanisms need to be considered for such a situation.

Couples worry about the need for both personal and physical space for themselves and the live-in relative. Furthermore, all family members wonder how they will adjust to and accept each additional member of the household. One of the women in our group, whose fiance's father lives in his home commented, "I really love Al, but I don't care much for Al's dad. I have real concerns about him living with us."

Feelings and concerns regarding the acceptance of additional family members, as well as the concern for the needs of frail, elderly relatives, should be shared by remarrying couples. Couples might want to pursue further information and assistance on how to cope lovingly and respectfully with this sometimes difficult situation.

Conclusion

Money, homes, relatives, and pets can enrich or sabotage a second marriage. With planning, perseverance, prayer, and humor, all can be managed so that these issues do not permanently cloud marital harmony.

In our culture, heavy emphasis is placed on money matters. Almost all our couples say that money presents a problem in their changing economic security that must be addressed. However, we encourage couples not to lose sight of the wealth available to us that is free. God gifts us with the beauty in all that surrounds us. We have but to look at a rose, view a mountain blanketed in snow, contemplate the rhythm and power of the ocean, or look into our lover's eyes to see the richness of God's gifts. Christian couples try to keep a perspective of the goodness of God's world even as they must remain practical in their pursuit of economic security for themselves and their families. We remind couples to be grateful for all that they have and not let their need for, or attachment to, money grow beyond their vision of the abundant gifts that are already theirs. We ask also that couples remember to share their abundance with those less fortunate.

Finances
WORKSHEET

Privately answer the questions, or respond to the statements with *Agree* or *Disagree*. Then share with your partner.

1. We should keep a monthly record of our income and expenses.

2. We are in agreement about who will handle the monthly budget and money matters.

3. One or both of us have some outstanding debts that worry me.

4. We should never buy on credit, only use cash.

5. I want credit cards of my own and will be responsible for their payments.

6. We agree on how we will handle our savings, our debts, our budget.

7. I want all our individual debts paid off before we marry.

8. I expect to pay for my children's education.

9. We should have a joint checking account to cover the household budget only.

10. I am confident that our income will cover our expenses.

11. I don't want to report to my partner every time I spend money.

12. I am concerned about my partner's ability to handle money.

13. My partner's child support payments should come out of his/her income, not mine.

14. We should put all child support income into the family general fund.

15. All my family inheritances and heirlooms should be in both our names.

16. Each of us should have a separate money account of our own to spend as we choose.

17. All assets/money gained from my previous marriage should remain in my name.

18. I am worried that we do not have enough life or medical insurance.

19. I have medical, dental, life insurance.

20. We should be the primary beneficiaries of each other's insurance policies.

21. I expect to remain financially independent after I marry.

22. Three important financial goals I have are . . .

23. I usually spend _____ on Christmas/birthday gifts for my children/parents/friends.

24. I have made a list of my assets/liabilities and my income/expenses and shared them with my partner.

25. Name one long-term financial goal on which you both agree.

26. We should each make a will.

27. Imagine you won the $5 million lottery. List five specific items your would purchase or things you would do for yourself. Name one item you would purchase for your partner.

28. I want to check into a premarital agreement.

29. I am comfortable with my partner's career and career goals.

30. I do not feel satisfied with my job/career.

31. In case of a transfer or job change, my career should come first.

32. We are in agreement about our future goals and ambitions.

33. We have made plans about where we will live after marriage.

34. We should sell our individual houses and buy a house together.

35. We should move into my house, sell my partner's house, and put the money in a joint savings account.

36. My partner should put his/her house in both our names.

37. We should get rid of our individual furniture and buy new furniture.

38. Some household items I want to keep are . . .

39. We should combine our furniture.

40. I want us to buy a new bed for our bedroom.

41. I want us both to be involved in the decorating and maintaining of our home.

42. We have discussed how we will divide household tasks and responsibilities.

43. I like to do the cooking.

44. I like to do the yard work.

45. One household task I really dislike doing is . . .

46. One household task I really enjoy doing is . . .

47. I have _____ pets. They are . . .

48. I cannot stand pets.

49. I feel we are rushing into marriage before we are ready.

Additional Comments:

*T*he more we are invested in people the less money we need. . . . The possessions we purchase are valuable and useful only if they are prized less than those gifts which have been freely given. The presence of another person and the love of a child, the grace of God and the sacraments of Christ, the seasons of the year and the stars in the heavens, faith and friendship, music and poetry give life human shape and substance. . . . A certain distance from possessions enhances our humanity and enables us to appreciate the worth of others.[3]

— Anthony Padovano
Love and Destiny:
Marriage as God's Gift

CHAPTER 5

Intimacy

---

*L*ove is patient and kind; it is not jealous or conceited or proud; love is not ill-mannered or selfish or irritable; love does not keep a record of wrongs; love is not happy with evil, but is happy with the truth. Love never gives up; and its faith, hope, and patience never fail.

— *1 Corinthians 13:4–8*

I was standing outside a conference room at the University of Notre Dame, soaking in the warm July sunshine, when a gentleman walked up to me to comment on the remarriage workshop I had just given.

> I agree with what you said in there about remarriage, but I have a problem. Judy and I have been going together for several years now and we are very much in love. However, whenever we discuss marriage, I panic. After my first wife betrayed and left me nine years ago, I struggled with that personal failure and it took me years to develop a sense of freedom and self-worth. Now, I am afraid to commit my life to another person so permanently again. I love Judy very much and I want to be close to her, but I am afraid of another divorce. I also worry I will lose the sense of personal identity and independence I have developed over these past years.

Although I did not know this man who spoke so frankly of his love relationship, his story echoes the story of many divorced persons who choose to "live in" a relationship rather than enter into another marriage.

Intimacy

Marital intimacy is a close, deep, thorough relationship with another involving one's total self — mind, body, and soul. Once betrayed by divorce, we frequently fear another abiding lifelong commitment. We worry about another rejection or the loss of our own autonomy and identity, especially if it has been won at the high emotional cost of divorce. We fear becoming emotionally dependent upon another, being smothered, or being rejected in the relationship. We fear the compromises and considerations of another that marriage requires. Repeating painful mistakes and the guilt that accompanies it causes us anxiety. The bitter taste of pain and anger from the past marital failure may still consume us. The dream of living "happily ever after" is shattered and disillusionment may sabotage our hope of ever finding true love in marriage. We wonder if a lifetime of love with one person is even possible. In our push-pull with intimacy, our yearnings for relationship battle with our fears and worries about the consequences and responsibilities of such relationships.

Many divorced persons who harbor these fears sit on the fence in new caring relationships, postponing the commitment to marriage to their partner. Others avoid the intimacy of close relationships altogether by frequently changing dating partners after the passion is spent, never allowing anyone to get too close. Avoiding intimacy reduces the risk of pain and rejection, the loss of control in our lives; it also closes the door to the riches that only the intimacy of a lifelong love can offer.

Intimacy, frequently reduced to the genital sexual aspect of a relationship, encompasses a much broader meaning. It is not limited to, nor does it necessarily include, sexual union or even marriage. It is a deep, strong attachment between persons whose lives are interdependent, including deep liking and/or loving. There is expectation for the relationship to endure and there is the capacity to highly reward and hurt each other. We can have these very close, satisfying relationships with our children, spouses, friends, and relatives. Intimacy takes many shapes: sex, a smile, a shared joke, a family ritual, a kiss, a touch, even a certain inflection of voice. With respect to marriage, however, we most often associate intimacy with love-making. Yet, without other particular qualities that enrich the intimate relationship, the love-making can be empty or only fleetingly satisfactory.

The very essence of intimacy in marriage requires accommodation, acceptance, compromise, the willingness to place someone else's welfare before one's own, and the willingness to live with and accept another's limitations while allowing that other to discover and accept our own inadequacies. It invites in-depth communication, whereby we share our hopes, our dreams, our fears, our views, and our values. It demands that we provide an atmosphere of loving acceptance as we listen to our spouse's fears and joys without judgment and criticism. It requires trust, truthfulness, open-mindedness, flexibility, and the inherent belief that each of us is lovable and capable.

Intimacy invites the risk of reconnecting, of becoming transparent. Frequently, one partner responds more openly, while the other hides in a shell waiting to be gently drawn forth from that secure place. It asks that mature people learn to live with and work within the ebb and flow, the hills and valleys that are always part of any marital relationship, rather than seeking outside stimulation such as work, TV, social activities or affairs when the marriage becomes boring or is in trouble.

Love makes us vulnerable and when we are vulnerable, we get hurt. When we protect ourselves from hurt, we also insulate ourselves against the loving acceptance that closeness with others can bring to our lives. C.S. Lewis writes eloquently about love in *The Four Loves*:

> There is no safe investment. To love at all is to be vulnerable. Love anything, and your heart will certainly be wrung and possibly be broken. If you want to make sure of keeping it intact, you must give your heart to no one, not even to an animal. Wrap it carefully round with hobbies and little luxuries; avoid all entanglements; lock it up safe in the casket or coffin of your selfishness. But in that casket — safe, dark, motionless, airless — it will change. It will not be broken; it will become unbreakable, impenetrable, irredeemable. The alternative to tragedy, or at least to the risk of tragedy, is damnation. The only place outside Heaven where you can be perfectly safe from all the dangers and perturbations of love is Hell.[1]

Intimacy begins with a healthy self-confidence and self-esteem, usually established early in life. I need to believe in my own goodness within my own imperfect humanity. If I don't, I will find it very difficult to accept someone else's imperfections. Moreover, I may not believe that someone else can accept an imperfect me.

Self-esteem leads to friendship, and friendship is an excellent foundation for marriage. Many of our second married couples talk of a friendship that blossomed into love. Anita and Robert met through a church potluck. Anita tells their story:

> Bob and I first met at a church social. Somehow our conversation locked onto our love for skiing. Neither one of us was looking for another partner at the time because we were quite busy raising children; he had a boy and a girl, I had a son. A few months later, when our parish ski group announced a planning meeting for the winter trips, we met again. We both joined the committee and became friends. It wasn't until a year later that we began more serious dating. We married six months later.

When friends eventually become lovers and marry, they speak of the comfort of the second relationship, not always apparent or present in the first marriage. They enjoy each other's company and bond on many levels.

I invited a remarried couple, Bob, an attorney, and Carol, a secretary, to speak to one of our remarriage groups. They were also friends before they became romantically involved. They have been married eight years and have worked hard to bond their relationship, especially since they each brought children into the second marriage. When I asked them to speak on the meaning of intimacy in their relationship, they responded:

> "For us," began Carol, "intimacy is closeness, being able to share our deepest feelings, concerns, our fears, knowing that we will not hold or use these things against each other. We enjoy similar interests, especially cycling, which brought us together. We have conflicts but we rely on our commitment and our friendship, along with our track record of honesty with each other, even when it hurts."
>
> "Our intimacy includes the sexual love we share," added Bob. "As our relationship has deepened over these years, our sex life has also become richly satisfying. Our friendship and love outside the bedroom directly affects the quality of our love-making in the bedroom."

All intimate relationships include people who are different. A friend, George, and his twenty-five-year-old son, Chuck, had one of those "father/son" talks one day while painting the living room in preparation for Chuck's forthcoming wedding.

"Dad," began Chuck, "I wonder sometimes about Barbara and I. We love each other but we argue seriously sometimes. I wonder whether we will become unhappy and maybe divorce. How did you and mom work out your differences?"

"Well," said George thoughtfully, "we worked them out by talking — sometimes arguing — often by just accepting our differences rather than trying to change each other. Although in our twenty-nine years together we have become more compatible, we are still very different. Some of our differences we have never resolved and probably never will. We just accept them, sometimes reluctantly, as part of the person we love.

"For instance, you know how I still get irritated when your mother insists on doing all the cooking without asking for help and then complains about it later; that is your mother. I've learned that she will probably never change, and so I accept it. When we were younger, we argued about it often.

"You know how your mother gets upset with me when I take so long on a project. Yet, she recognizes that this is how I do things and if I haven't changed in the last twenty-nine years, I'm not about to now.

"We are very close, your mother and I, even though we don't always agree. We support each other and love each other and all of you kids very much.

"Son, everyone has good and not so good qualities. In our marriage, we try to focus on one another's good qualities, and accept or learn to live with the qualities that irritate us. It takes time and we have had many serious arguments, but acceptance is the key, son, at least it is for us."

Love and Marriage Complications

Dating

Love begins with dating. Each of us comes to the dating scene, whether in high school or later in life with an ideal marriage and marriage partner in our unconscious if not our conscious mind. This internal ideal reflects our value system shaped by our parents and families, our schools, our churches, and our culture. When we are attracted to someone, we project onto that person the important things we want or expect in our ideal life partner. Those qualities are usually present only in our projection, not necessarily in the person on whom we project them. Sometime later, when we see our partner more clearly, we wonder how and when they changed.

Dr. Michael Cavanagh, a professor of psychology at University of San Francisco, in a 1974 column written for *The Monitor*, the San Francisco archdiocesan Catholic newspaper (no longer in print), described the three phases of dating: infatuation, objectivity and honesty, and altruism.

Phase One: Infatuation. When we are attracted to someone, we dust off and bring out our best social behaviors. We put on our "dating mask" as we remember our "pleases" and "thank-you's"; we bring gifts; we listen to the other — enraptured — for hours; we open doors and help the other with coats, we dress in our best and flirt; and, we are polite and accommodating, nearly always focusing on the other's desires and the excitement we feel. We are attracted physically and emotionally, and we do everything we can to make a good impression, to encourage the other to like us, and to show how much we like them. We think we have finally found our one true love — our soul mate — who truly loves and understands us. We feel totally in tune with the other. In this rarefied, intoxicating air of infatuation, we believe this perfect match will last forever.

Phase Two: Objectivity and Honesty. In the second phase, usually after we have been dating a while, we begin to notice little things that annoy us. He stutters, she is often tardy; he drives a little too fast, she talks too much; he's a picky eater, she's a poor housekeeper; she loves sports and exercise, he prefers the arts. We have differences of opinion on politics, or raising children, or family relationships. One likes horror movies, the other enjoys romantic comedies. She prefers camping, he loves lavish cruises. As we get to know each other and feel more secure in the relationship, we begin to act more naturally, gradually removing our dating masks. Sometimes we show our anger, or disappointment, or moodiness. We react to annoying imperfections or behavior in the other. Since we are more relaxed, our true nature and values begin to show. At this stage, there may be some disagreements and disillusionment as some unreal expectations disintegrate and the person appears to have changed. Sometimes real fights break out bringing the relationship to the status of make-up or break-up. At this point, some relationships break up in anger and bitterness, others with grace. Later, the relationship may take on the aspect of friendship rather than love, or, the individuals may never see each other again.

Phase Three: Altruism. If the couple reconciles and manages to steer through the roadblocks of reality and sobering objectivity of the second phase and the individuals are still attracted to one another, the love bond deepens. Gradually, the sole excitement of sexual attraction that characterizes phase one changes to soul excitement, deep love, and respect of one person for another. Individuals accommodate each other's personalities into their couple bond. Each person allows the other to grow and each shares in the joy and pain of that growth. There may still be rough edges in their bonding as in most enduring relationships, but, as the couple negotiates through their conflict, it becomes a steppingstone toward their personal and couple growth in intimacy and love. It is at the end of the second phase and at the beginning of this third phase that marital commitment appropriately begins through engagement to marry and/or marriage itself.

According to Dr. Cavanagh, many people decide to marry in the first phase of the relationship when excitement and attraction are high, and reality is low. After marriage, these spouses unexpectedly experience the reality of the second phase. One morning one spouse wakes up and says to the other, "You've changed. You're not the person I married!" This crisis can lead to the decline of the marital relationship which may, even after many years, end in divorce, or, it can lead to re-evaluation and recommitment to the changing relationship.

Dr. Cavanagh believes that a couple's decision for marriage would better occur toward the end of the second stage, when the individuals are more realistic about their partner and their relationship. No relationship, or marriage, or marriage partner is perfect. Marriage, like life, is a process of ongoing change facilitated by the changing individuals. About the time when someone says "Now, we've finally got it together," everything shifts! Therefore, upon entering this lifelong commitment, we need to be aware of our own limitations and those of the other. We need to learn that spouses and marital relationships must grow and change, not remain static, if they are going to be life-giving and successful. This necessitates flexibility, periodical re-evaluation, and re-negotiation, usually at crisis times, throughout the life of the marriage.

Dr. Cavanagh concludes his column by writing:

A factor that complicates matters [about these phases] is that almost everyone who has ever married or entered into a permanent love relationship was convinced that he or she had indeed grown through phase two and into three; that each was objective and honest and could focus on the other.

Formerly married individuals who date usually experience these same stages especially as they approach a more serious relationship. However, because of the failure of the first marriage, many are cautious. Reality sets in earlier and the couple may remain in the second phase for a long time out of fear that a new marriage may also collapse.

Mature Love

In a workshop handout on "Our Love History," Dr. Cavanagh describes the four stages of development of mature love:

Stage 1. Infancy; signified by the statement, "I love things that make me feel good" (food, sleep, thumb, erogenous areas, warmth, soothing sounds, safety).

Stage 2. About age eighteen months; signified by "I love you for what you can do for me."

Stage 3. About age fourteen; signified by romantic love: "I love you for what you can do for me," in the sense of "I'll scratch your back if you will scratch mine." This is different from the previous stage in that giving is part of the getting.

Stage 4. Mature love; signified by "I love you for who you are." Giving is out of love, and the well-being of the other is the primary concern.

Dr. Cavanagh indicates that each of the stages partially prepares one for mature love. He states:

Loving something (food and one's body) must precede loving somebody (mother); loving parents must precede loving non-caretakers and siblings, then same-sexed friends, then opposite-sexed friends. Loving me must precede loving you for who you are. Not one of these steps can be skipped or rushed.

When couples enter a second marriage, especially if they have prepared well, their expectations are more reasonable and they tend to have better, happier marriages. Those who enter a second marriage while still in the first dating phase may be mesmerized by their passion, may unconsciously be looking for a relationship out of a dependency need, or may be rebounding from the first marriage failure. Most rebound marriages include the seeds of failure within because individuals bring substantial excess baggage, such as unfinished bitterness and anger, from the previous marriage and divorce into the second union. Sometimes individuals marry a transitional person — one who fulfills the nurturing needs of the wounded heart — but, after healing takes place, the transitional figure may no longer fit as an appropriate life partner, and the marriage fails.

Sidney J. Harris, in one of his syndicated columns entitled, "The true test of love reposes in tranquility," wrote of marriage as a resting place: "Marriage . . . does not change people; it merely unmasks them. It strips off the strangeness, the glamour, the appearance of strength, the fascination of novelty." He further quotes St. Bernard of Clairvaux: "'We find rest in those we love, and we provide a resting place in ourselves for those who love us.'" Mr. Harris concludes:

> . . . two persons have to rest easily with each other, or the ordinary abrasions of family life will begin to wear away the relationship, leaving little but wistfulness and puzzlement and, eventually, resentment that the reality is nothing like the romance. . . .
>
> A resting place is what we need as we grow older. A place not to gaze at each other in mutual fascination, but to look out at the world together from much the same angle of vision. A harbor, a shelter, a refuge, a source of nourishment and support. This is not what creates a marriage, but this is what sustains it.[2]

Mutual Projection

In an article entitled "Why Love Is So Complicated," published in Notre Dame Magazine, C. William Tageson writes of the two general ways in which social scientists have described attraction between people. One is characterized by the timeworn phrase "birds of a feather flock together," which means that people who have similar backgrounds, core values, and life preferences are attracted to each other. The other common phrase is "opposites attract." Obviously this refers to the fact that introverts may be attracted to extroverts, creative types to intellectual types, and so on. Although these views oppose each other, both are found to be true, sometimes in the same marriage.

Mr. Tageson refers to the dynamics between couples as a mutual projection system. He states:

> We humans have a tendency to project unconsciously onto others what we have repressed or failed to develop in ourselves. We explore vicariously, through the behavior of another person, those aspects of ourselves which we have lacked the opportunity or the courage to develop.[3]

We cannot expect the other person to make up for qualities we lack. Therefore, we must reclaim our projections on others and ". . . develop within [ourselves] to some appropriate degree, those qualities once enjoyed only vicariously through [our] spouse."

He indicates that relationship between opposites can be either a source for couple growth or the seed of the relationship's destruction. The reclamation process in this type of relationship often comes during a crisis. A similar view is expressed in the following lines:

> I often wonder what made us fall in love with each
>   other.
> We are so different from each other.
> Our strengths and weaknesses are so different.
> Our ways of approaching things are so different.
> Our personalities are so different.
> Yet our love continues to grow and grow.
> Perhaps the differences we have add to the excitement
>   of our relationship,
> and I know that both of us as a team are stronger than
>   either of us alone.
> We are basically different from each other but we have
>   so many feelings and emotions in common.
> And it really doesn't matter why we fell in love.

All that matters to me is that we continue to love each
other forever.[4]

— *Susan Polis Schutz*

In my first marriage, my husband's and my values, our perspectives, our positive outlook on life exhibited the "birds of feather"
quality. We rarely quarreled. However, I was a shy, reflective introvert and emotionally dependent upon my husband for self-
confidence and self-esteem, particularly in public situations. My
husband was not a self-reflective or self-revealing person. He was
the extrovert — a public, humorous, party personality and apparently very independent. I admired those traits in him, especially because I felt so inadequate. I thrived on being in his shadow because
it made me feel good. Secretly, I wanted to be just like him. Over
the years, I developed many of those qualities as I watched him
and sometimes imitated him. Although our personality traits were
quite opposite in the beginning, the dynamics of our personalities
did change. As I became more extroverted and independent, he
became more introverted and somewhat threatened by my growing
self-confidence. I was no longer the "same person" he had married twenty years before. At the crisis point of our marriage, we
could have taken the opportunity to re-evaluate and re-negotiate
our relationship. If we could have worked with a counselor, been
willing to "hang in there" through the difficult times, and tried
to understand what was happening, we would have been greatly
enriched by the process and probably would still be together today.
Unfortunately that was not to be.

In my present marriage, Larry and I encounter many differences. We test out opposites in three out of the four catagories of
the Myers-Briggs personality inventory. He is the introvert, I am
the extrovert; he focuses on specific problems, I tend to generalize
(I see the forest, he sees the tree); I tend to be more impatient,
organized and decisive, he prefers to follow the spontaneity and
flow of life. We disagree more frequently because of our individual
characteristics and independence, but we deeply love each other
and we respect our marital commitment and individuality. We re-
negotiate often! Our differences strengthen and enrich our relationship. I have learned some measure of patience from him, he
has learned some organizational skills from me. During the ten

years we have been married, we have become more compatible and have experienced increased satisfaction in our journey together, even though we still maintain our own distinct individuality and identity.

Kahlil Gibran writes provocatively of marital differences in "On Marriage" in *The Prophet*:

> Let there be spaces in your togetherness,
> And let the winds of the heavens dance between you.
> Love one another, but make not a bond of love:
> Let it rather be a moving sea between the shores of
>   your souls.
> Fill each other's cup but drink not from one cup.
> Give one another of your bread but eat not from the
>   same loaf.
> Sing and dance together and be joyous, but let each
>   one of you be alone,
> Even as the strings of a lute are alone though they
>   quiver with the same music.
> Give your hearts, but not into each other's keeping
> For only the hand of Life can contain your hearts.
> And stand together yet not too near together:
> For the pillars of the temple stand apart,
> And the oak tree and the cypress grow not in each
>   other's shadow.[5]

Marriage

Many marriages fail due to the neglect of the couple bond. A perception abounds that once the couple states their "I do's" the relationship is somehow protected against failure and will continue without effort, nourished by love alone. The high divorce rate contradicts that myth. Relationships need to be nurtured in order to develop the long-term attachment that occurs as the intense passion subsides.

Marriages don't grow and deepen on their own. It takes work, especially in second marriages, where stepparenting, finances, and possible interference from former spouses can strain the couple bond to the breaking point. Many couples who are succeeding in second marriages comment that they work hard to keep it healthy. One friend stated that if she had worked as hard in her first marriage as she does now, it might not have failed. Sometimes it takes the experience of a failed marriage to understand how to live successfully with another person.

The building blocks for a successful future marriage can some-times be found in the ashes of the past marital failure. Hopefully, as we grow older and evaluate our life's journey, especially our past marriage, we gain insight and understanding of ourselves and our value system, our weaknesses and strengths, and the kind of person that we can best live with for a lifetime. Preparation for the second marriage takes time and begins with the previous divorce. Time is needed to:

♦ Complete the grieving process and mine the riches of the past experience. If one has not discovered and identified the gifts within the painful upheaval of divorce, one probably is not ready to enter into another union.

♦ Develop a personal adult autonomy and a style of single, independent living. One should be able to say that he or she does not need marriage to feel good and be happy. Some-times people are so desperate to marry again that they refuse to see the warning signs of disaster in a new relationship until after the marriage. A second divorce usually occurs within two to four years and the individual suffers even more trauma in such a situation.

♦ Make peace, as far as possible. End the war between you and your former spouse so that one does not carry anger and bitterness from one marriage to the other. Maintain the responsibilities from the first marriage, i.e., support pay-ments, custody arrangements, and shared parenting of the children of the former marriage.

Romancing the Couple Bond

The new couple bond is very fragile. Once the courtship ends and marriage begins, the courtship dance of flowers, candy, and special romantic dates declines — especially in second marriages when couples often must "honeymoon in a crowd."

A difficult task for every couple with children living at home is to work out their own marital adjustment, while coping with the stress of stepparent adjustment. When there are stepchildren, this new bond must compete with other parent-child bonds that are longer and stronger. A concerted effort must be made by both partners to nurture their love. Quality time alone must be regularly planned into their life and each spouse should contribute to that effort.

Liesel and Tom, who attended our workshops, shared with us how they keep romance alive in their second marriage:

> We take turns planning special dates for each other several times a year. We set the date on the calendar and plan as the weekend approaches. Sometimes we surprise each other. Nothing is allowed to interfere with that date, short of a real emergency.

Larry and I picked up on their idea and have set aside special dates for each other as well. One time, Larry took me to San Francisco. After some window shopping, he led me to the theater to see *Fiddler on the Roof*, a play I had been dying to see. It was an exciting surprise and we had a wonderful evening following the play.

Another time, when finances were really tight while he was going to school to complete a degree, I had $100 with which to work. I planned a surprise weekend for him by taking him to a movie, then preparing a steak dinner on Saturday. On Sunday I asked him to pack a bag and we went on a get-away weekend at the Marriott with a coupon that included dinner and breakfast. We finished off the weekend on Monday at a local club's happy hour with a glass of wine and hors d'oeuvres. I had $2.37 left and we had a spectacular weekend together. Since then we always plan a special weekend away within two weekends of our wedding anniversary each year. We either plan it together or take turns planning it. Frequently, we surprise one another.

In most families, one person does most of the social planning. When spouses take turns planning a special outing, each one thinks about the other and what will please them both as he or she makes all the arrangements. The recipient partner feels terrific because his or her interests are taken into consideration and the relationship is valued.

Some other suggestions coming from our rich resource of second married couples are listed below:

♦ Joel and Emily explore each other's worlds as they plan special events for each other. Sometimes, they plan an activity to share an interest. For instance, Joel is a football fan so Emily purchased tickets to see one of his favorite teams. Joel, in turn, took Emily to the ballet, even though he does not care for ballet. A new twist might be that the spouse share a special interest with his or her partner. (He takes her to a football game and she takes him to the ballet.)

♦ One woman set up a romantic pursuit for their anniversary. When her husband arrived home from work, he found a note on the kitchen table in the form of a rhymed clue that directed him to the next destination. After several stops at some of their favorite spots and at cooperative friends' homes, where additional clues awaited him, he arrived at the hotel room she had rented for a get-away weekend where she warmly greeted him. Needless to say, they had a marvelous weekend.

♦ The husband of another couple kidnapped his wife right after work one Friday and took her away for a surprise weekend. He, of course, made all the arrangements for necessary sitters and preparations for the journey.

♦ Another husband sends flowers to his wife at her workplace several times a year for no particular reason except to say "I love you."

♦ A wife surprised her husband one morning with a car full of balloons saying "I love you."

♦ Another couple with limited finances and young stepchildren created a way to spend special time together without the cost of a babysitter. They take turns planning a late candlelight dinner at home. The one in charge sends the other an invitation to "Dinner at Chez Moi," and sets up the whole meal, which includes feeding and putting the children to bed early. Sometimes he brings food from outside; sometimes she prepares a special meal at home. They recognize the value of building and supporting a quality couple bond.

♦ Recently, a talk-show host told his audience about how he and his wife of six years live very structured, individual, busy lives. Each travels a good deal so they don't see each other often during the week. To avoid becoming "strangers in the night" they set aside Saturday morning from 10:00 to 12:00 as their quality time. Phones are taken off the hook, and they allow no interruptions. During the week each makes a list of things they want to discuss or share. If there is nothing to share, they use that time for romance. In this manner, they demonstrate that they truly value their relationship.

♦ Another couple living with their several step-children in snow country sent their children out to shovel the snow on their long driveway in mid-afternoon so that they could have at least twenty minutes of intimate time together.

Alice confessed, "In only ten minutes, one of the children returned to the house, thus shortchanging our time together." She giggled. "It got to the point that we asked ourselves, 'How quickly can we do it?'"

Leisure time and recreation are essential elements for mental, physical, and emotional well-being. They provide the opportunity for couples to re-create their intimacy and reinforce their couple bond as well as relax. The activities a couple chooses do not have to be expensive. A day away at the park or a drive in the country or along the beach with a picnic lunch can energize their romance as well as an expensive trip to a hotel or bed-and-breakfast inn for the weekend.

In our western society, we often "work hard" at our recreation or vacationing. A vacation may provide a change of place, but not always a change of pace. People frequently come home from vacations or leisure activities harried or exhausted instead of relaxed and refreshed. Couples should plan activities that they enjoy doing together and that offer some quiet couple time just to talk, muse, dream, and share stories together — intimate time — rather than following a frenzied timetable that leaves them weary.

Taking a walk together each day can not only add quality to the couple bond, but also provide pleasant, healthy exercise as well. If there are custodial children in the household, we suggest couples plan time alone — each day, if possible, or at least weekly — and a minimum of one quality day away every four to six weeks in which they are not allowed to talk about problems, work, or kids. They need to focus on each other and their couple love. Usually family or close friends can be relied upon for babysitting purposes, especially if there is an exchange of babysitting; otherwise, a babysitting co-op might be sought out. Couples with busy schedules often set a date in advance even though the planning for their special time will begin later.

Diane and Lawson easily fell into a nice pattern of sharing for a half hour or so at the end of dinner, after the children left the table.

"It just happened," says Diane, "and it's a time we relax together and catch up on each other's day. We have been enjoying this for the last two years. Even our children respect this time we spend together since they rarely interrupt."

Regardless of how or what each couple does in providing special treasured moments for themselves, this regular quality time surely will enhance their couple bond and their love for each other. The key here is quality time which includes:

♦ regularity and priority of the commitment;

♦ mutuality (taking turns);

♦ occasional surprises.

Another way couples build a loving bond is by performing simple tasks for each other. Because they love one another, they may already do such things, but may never have told their spouse. In our house, Larry makes the bed every morning (which is a treat for me), and I get up with him at 5:30 a.m. to make his breakfast and his bag lunch (which gives him a little more "sleeping" time). We do these things out of love for each other.

Another couple, Kevin and Marie, told us about their gifts of love:

"I bring her coffee into the bathroom in the morning so that she can have a cup when she steps out of the shower," says Kevin.

"Kevin hates to fold his underwear," adds Marie, "so I fold it for him. Now there are times . . ." chuckles Marie, "when I would rather cut his underwear to shreds, and Kevin would like to throw the coffee in the bathroom, but we don't, because even though we are angry at the moment, we do value the core of our relationship, our mutual love."

Couples can share with each other what they already are doing for the other out of love. Each spouse could also list things they would like to have done by the other. Maybe it would be putting the cap back on the toothpaste, or sharing a glass of wine before dinner, or giving a back, neck, or foot massage, or helping with dishes, cooking, or yard work. One woman puts love notes in her husband's bag lunch. Another couple makes an effort to pay sincere compliments to each other regularly. These small love-gifts enhance intimacy and communication between husband and wife and demonstrate that each cherishes their relationship, even in difficult times.

A few years ago I read "The Invitation to Live" by Ardis Whitman in *Reader's Digest*, April 1972. She expressed her understanding of relationship in the following excerpt:

> We help or hinder one another, summoning one another to be and grow, or to surrender and retreat, influencing one another as sun and frost influence a green field.
>
> In *The Transparent Self*, psychotherapist Sidney Jourard claims that this process goes on all the time, that we all constantly issue unique and powerful invitations to each other to live or die, to triumph or surrender. When I am with you I grow or diminish according to how you make me feel. And, in my turn, I invite you to live or to die simply by existing in your presence, by walking with you or retreating, by holding my hand to you or not holding it, by opening my heart to you or keeping it closed.
>
> If we would invite a person to live, we must accept the "otherness" of that person. We must hear out their dreams, not dismiss them with naysaying. Above all, we must see what is best in him (or her) and give it permission to be and grow. For growth is the very insignia of every living creature, the heart of the life process — life is a growing tree, not a statue.
>
> We live when we are true to ourselves, authentic in our feelings, responsive to our convictions; we live when we love, when we are involved in the lives of others, when we are committed and concerned; we live when we build and create, hope, suffer and rejoice. Life grows as it is spent.[6]

The Elephant in the Living Room

Johnny Carson interviewed a marriage counselor on his show a few years ago. When he asked the counselor what he thought was the cause of so much divorce, the counselor replied, "The elephant in the living room." After a few chuckles, Johnny asked him what he meant by that. The counselor replied, "If you had an elephant in your living room and nobody talked about it, wouldn't you say you had a problem?" The counselor continued by saying that communication is lacking in many troubled marriages. The "elephant in the living room" is any problem that one or both spouses are aware of but refuse to discuss.

Nearly all of our couples agree that lack of communication was a big contributing factor in the failure of their previous marriages, and they are anxious to learn new communication skills. They allude to the fact that the "elephants" in their previous relationships got so big that either one or both parties tried to pretend it did not exist until it was too late.

Of course the "elephant" does not go away when couples ignore it. In fact it usually grows larger the longer it is ignored. Sometimes, the "elephant" gets so enormous that there is no room for marital harmony and hospitality. Individual spouses may even perceive the "elephant" differently. Once they begin to share their differing perspectives of the problem and their feelings, they may discover that the issue can be resolved before it gets out of hand. A couple might open their discussion with, "I think there is an elephant in our living room that we need to talk about. . . ." One of our couples actually had a stuffed toy elephant and creatively decided to place it in the middle of their living room table as a signal that they had an issue to discuss. They felt it facilitated the opening of their discussion.

Communication is more than saying words. It is sharing at a deep level our feelings and concerns, our likes and dislikes, and what is bothering us. It is also listening to the concerns of our loved ones with our hearts and minds, without recrimination or judgment, a very difficult but essential ingredient to good communication. So often people talk quite well, but they listen poorly.

Good communication also includes creative problem solving and forgiveness. Couples sometimes question whether quarreling helps or hurts the relationship. Confronting and solving problems evokes frustration, guilt, anger, and fear. We do not want to suffer or risk being rejected, but when we learn how to manage family problems, we mature individually and in the relationship.

I like the way M. Scott Peck writes about problems in *The Road Less Traveled*:

> Problems are the cutting edge that distinguishes between
> success and failure. Problems call forth our courage and
> our wisdom; indeed they create our courage and wisdom.
> It is only because of problems that we grow mentally and
> spiritually.[7]

If the fighting is fair and the couple creatively work together to solve the problem in an atmosphere of love, consideration, and acceptance, even a very large "elephant" can be handled and sent on its way. To be willing to say "I'm sorry" or to accept another's offer of reconciliation stimulates healing the hurts and allows the couple to begin anew. To neglect the "elephant" is to neglect the relationship. When neglect sets in, the relationship can die. Successful problem solving and reconciliation enhance closeness and intimacy rather than hurt the relationship. Communication is the key that unlocks the door to that kind of intimacy.

If a couple finds themselves caught in the mire of a problem they are unable to clarify or resolve, they might seek out a therapist to assist them. Therapists say that if a couple comes in early enough and is willing to work at discovering a satisfying solution, problems can be successfully resolved. Unfortunately, many couples wait too long, allowing anger, resentment, and hurt to increase stress levels to the point where one or both spouses are unwilling to do what is necessary to achieve a workable solution. In such cases, even therapy is unsuccessful.

What is the elephant in your living room?

Sexual Intimacy

Sex is the peak physical expression of intimacy. It can be playful, casual, fun, loving, seductive, healing, and an intense, spiritual and emotional merging. Each of us brings different expectations about sex based on our upbringing and adult sexual history.

Reviewing how our parents did or did not reflect their love in the home as well as what we were taught by home, school, and church will give clues as to how and why we repress or express sexual intimacy the way we do. If parents were touching, playful, caring people, comfortable with their bodies and their female and male roles in the home, their adult children will probably reflect those positive qualities in their own adult life. If parents' behavior indicated sexuality should be hidden, that it was nasty, that bodies were bad, their adult children will also reflect the guilt associated with those negative images. If someone was subject to any kind of physical, psychological, or sexual abuse particularly as a child, his or her ability to respond freely and joyfully to sexual intimacy may be severely damaged. Frequently, the memory of abuse has been blocked but the negative response to sex has not. In such cases, therapy may be necessary to help clear the way for a healthy sexual response. Unless adults become aware through reading, therapy and/or personal experience of the goodness of our physical beings, body and soul, they will have a difficult time being comfortable with sexual intimacy.

Terrie, a young woman I met at one of the separated and divorced conferences, told me of her sexual history:

> As a child, I got lots of negative unspoken messages about sex not only from my parents, but also from church. Sex was this nasty thing that nice people don't do — except in marriage. It was difficult for me to switch from those programmed negative sexual values to positive ones on my first wedding night! I couldn't do it. My negative feelings about sex made our marriage nearly impossible. After a divorce, I went through months of therapy to wade through a lifetime of guilt.

Sometimes, in former marriages, there have been negative sexual experiences that can impact a second marriage. Although it is important not to compare spouses, the couple must take time to demonstrate in words and deeds what they each find satisfying and pleasurable. Few people have equal or similar affection needs. Therefore, spouses should share their expectations and desires.

As with everything else in a second marriage, sex will also be different. You will learn to adjust to each other's styles and rhythms. Be sure to give clear messages. Include spontaneity in your sex life. Each of you take responsibility for helping the other feel satisfied. When both of you are able to express your needs greater satisfaction occurs. There needs to be a mutuality of giving and receiving in bed as well as anywhere else. If there is sex dysfunction, seek professional assistance to learn the causes how to become functional. Even in the effort to develop satisfaction, you can become very close.

Remember too, that sexual intimacy can be a caring or holding hands, or cuddling. Sometimes that is what want — just to be touched and hugged. Sidney Simon, in his book *Caring, Feeling, Touching*, calls it skin hunger. He says:

> [Touching is the] most basic of all forms of human commu-
> nication. It is communication that speaks without words. It
> delivers the most assuring message that can be exchanged
> between persons: "I am here, you are here, and we care."[8]

Touching is an affirmation of our physical selves, and many studies indicate that it is absolutely necessary to our physical well-being. Mr. Simon further quotes the late Florida University psychologist Sidney Jourard, who wrote:

> I think that body-contact has the function of confirming
> one's bodily being. We live in an age of "unembodiment,"
> or "disembodiment," and I believe that the experience
> of being touched enlivens our bodies and brings us back
> into them.

Although some people say that the only good thing about their marriage is their sex life, most happily married couples state that their healthy relationship outside the bedroom greatly enhances their sex life. They have given up the freedom and variety of singleness for the rich rewards of coupleness. The whole of their lives — the giving and receiving, the mutuality of their love and care for each other, their sharing in the push-pull of intimacy — work together to create their enduring relationships.

Conclusion

Intimacy, in all its styles, is at the heart of a good relationship. ﹍gh difficult to attain, it is important to the growth of your ﹍nd. It is worked out over years of living, loving, suffering, ﹍ laughing together. We encourage you to become a ﹍ortive, cooperative, problem solving team. Ask your-﹍ am I willing to give, to endure, to struggle in ﹍ marriage dreams come true?" Don't take your ﹍ marriage for granted. Develop an attitude of ﹍es you must put your own needs on hold ﹍'s wishes and vice versa. Share decision-﹍cus on what is good in your partner ﹍ marriage requires an investment of ﹍e prepared for change, for ups and downs, for sadness and gladness, and know that the stronger the basic unit of the family — the couple bond — the stronger the system — the total family.

As you conclude this chapter, may I suggest that you write a love letter to your partner today? You also might consider gifting your partner with a letter at the beginning of each new anniversary year.

Happiest Couples

Demonstrate openness, flexibility, honesty, and trust;

Enjoy love and commitment;

Spend significant quality time together;

Share common goals;

Do not blame, discount, or put each other down;

Talk about their feelings and concerns;

Listen to each other with love;

Solve problems creatively;

Say "I'm sorry";

Seek outside help when necessary;

Rejoice in each other's strengths;

Help with each other's struggles;

Promote each other's welfare;

Recognize and accept differences in perspective rather than determining right or wrong;

See their differences as a source of mutual growth;

Agree on how to handle finances;

Find sex mutually satisfying;

'are household responsibilities;

ht expect a perfect marriage or marriage partner;

ent each other often;

ther lots of hugs and kisses;

ey preach;

base for their relationship;

h love and respect;

umor.

Intimacy
WORKSHEET

Privately answer the questions, or respond to statements with *Agree* or *Disagree*. Then share with your partner.

1. Define the difference between love, sex, and intimacy.

2. I really enjoy being with my partner most of the time.

3. Sharing my deepest feelings about what is important to me is one way of intimacy.

4. Friendship is essential to a healthy marriage.

5. I feel closest to my partner when . . .

6. I feel very distant from my partner when . . .

7. Intimacy involves being mutually sensitive to one another's needs and desires.

8. I have grown up with good feelings about sex.

9. Some of the attitudes/events/information that influenced my sexual values are . . .

10. For me, sex and love are different things.

11. Intimacy can be attained without sexual intercourse.

12. Love-making is an art we can learn together.

13. In my first marriage, sexuality was a problem for me.

14. I received most of my information about sex from my parents.

15. Sexual intercourse is a good cure for a headache.

16. I feel comfortable discussing sexual matters/needs with my partner.

17. One of my fears about sex is . . .

18. The one question I would like to ask my partner about sex is . . .

19. I am bothered by the way my partner shows affection to me in public.

20. I am afraid of being sexually unsatisfying to my partner.

21. The thought of revealing my body to my partner makes me nervous.

22. I like the ways we show affection to each other.

23. One of the things I find physically attractive about my partner is . . .

24. A good way to work out problems between us is to make love.

25. The issue of premarital sex has caused me some conflict.

26. When I feel angry, hurt, or upset, I do not want to make love.

27. My partner should initiate sex.

28. I want my sexual relationship with my partner to be varied.

29. I am fearful that I might be sexually impotent/frigid.

30. I want my partner to tell me he/she loves me often.

31. Whatever we do to celebrate our marriage sexually is OK as long as we both find it acceptable and pleasurable.

32. What circumstances do you find most exciting sexually?

33. My partner should know what I want and need without my having to tell him/her.

34. It is my duty to respond to my partner sexually whenever he/she asks.

35. I expect to be fully satisfied whenever we make love.

36. My right in marriage is to have intercourse with my partner whenever I choose.

37. Sometimes I just want to be lovingly held or touched instead of intercourse.

38. I plan to continue our courtship and romance after marriage in the following ways . . .

39. I do not want to be compared to my partner's former spouse.

40. My partner respects my pursuit of my own interests, hobbies, or activities.

41. I am unhappy with one or more of my partner's interests, hobbies, or activities.

42. List in two columns: What do I expect to gain (benefits) when I marry? What do I expect to give up (losses) when I marry?

43. What are my rights, expectations, and duties in marriage?

44. Five things I really appreciate about my partner are . . .

45. We are able to maintain a sense of humor most of the time in our relationship.

46. List ten loving things you do for your partner to show your love.

47. List ten loving things your partner could do for you to show his/her love.

48. My favorite type of vacation is . . .

49. I am excited about my marriage to my partner.

50. Write a love letter to your partner.

Additional Comments:

To be truly happy in love a person must want unity, oneness, sharing. Sometimes this unity involves many things that are painful: honesty when you would rather lie a little, talking-out when you would rather pout, admitting embarrassing feelings when you would rather blame someone, standing there when you would rather run, admitting doubt when you would rather pretend certainty, and confronting when you would rather settle for peace at any price. None of these things which are among the just demands of love brings immediate peace and happiness, they bring immediate pain and struggle. Love works if we will work at it. The work of love is to achieve a total honesty and transparency, and these are very difficult attainments. . . .

If love is anything, it is a gradual process, the long round curve that must be carefully negotiated, not the sharp right angle turn that is made in an instant once and for all. A man or woman must set out upon a long journey and walk many miles to find the joys of love. They will have to pass through deep and dark forests and there will be many dangers. They will have to be careful of love as they are of few other things. Love will demand abstinence from all that might prove poisonous to love. Love will demand much courage, perseverance and self-discipline.

But the journey to love is the journey to the fullness of life. It is only in the experience of love that we can know ourselves, can love what we are and what we will become. It is only in the experience of love that we find the fullness of life that is the glory of God.[9]

—John Powell
The Secret of Staying in Love

CHAPTER 6

Religious Issues

*D*ear friends, if this is how God has loved us, then we should love one another. No one has ever seen God, but if we love one another, God lives in union with us and his love is made perfect in us.

— *1 John 4:11–12*

"Religion became one of the major sources of discontent in our marriage," says Marci, who is divorcing John after twenty years. "Even before Vatican II, we argued over birth control, Catholic school education for our children, our differing views on Catholic teaching, and my active parish work as a CCD teacher. We were both raised and educated in the church of the forties. John, a traditional Catholic, believes the 'right' approach to worship is through the quiet Latin mass. He misses the Latin hymns and the sense of awe and pageantry in the Latin liturgy. I tend to be more practical and open to the refreshing changes of Vatican II. I love the participatory approach to liturgy, the kiss of peace, the folk and upbeat music, and the energy and joyful prayerfulness of the eucharistic meal. John hates the new changes and resents my active participation in the parish. We have been attending separate liturgies for a long time. Recently, John began attending another church with a more fundamental approach. I have felt oppressed and rejected by him in these as well as other matters for so long that there is no love left."

Although John and Marci's religious disagreements are symptomatic of the major irreconcilable differences that permeated their entire marriage relationship, those quarrels certainly contributed to the marital breakdown. Their personalities and lifestyles clashed. John is closed to any new religious insights and objects to his wife following them. Marci flows more easily with life and wants to be

143

free to choose her own style without recriminations and judgments. During the passing years, their positions hardened and they now are unable to work out their differences. Although Marci entered counseling and encouraged John to join her, he refused. Even a session with their priest deteriorated into a major argument.

The power of love can transcend even major differences. Unfortunately, in John and Marci's situation, love was blocked by their lack of accommodation to each other's needs. To sum up, a person's style and practice of religious faith can negatively impact a marriage, even when both spouses are of the same religion!

We conclude *Once More With Love* with a discussion on religious issues for remarrieds. The previous five chapters focused on the stressful practical issues that most remarried couples face. This sixth one focuses on God as the center, the anchor, and the foundation of the permanent bond of love and commitment in Christian marriage. We will also cover the stages of faith and share some information on particular aspects of faith life, sacramental marriage, and annulment.

The more a couple grows in love, the more they resemble God. God is love and the source of strength that couples need to help them work out the stressful concerns of second marriage. Just as we bring our other histories to the marital union, we come to remarriage with a faith history. Our image of God, the core of our religious belief, begins early in life with our parent role models and early religious training.

Stages of Faith

When couples prepare to marry a second time, it is helpful to identify the specific stages of religious faith in their individual lives and to clarify their adult Christian roles and practices with each other. Then they can plan together how they will continue the journey as a couple while enriching their marital relationship through religious practices that are comfortable for both of them.

Rev. Richard J. Sweeney describes six stages of faith in his *Catholic Update* article "How God Invites Us to Grow."[1] He entitles them: imaginative faith, literal faith, group faith, personal faith, mystical faith, and sacrificial faith.

Imaginative faith forms in early childhood, up to about the age of seven. Mystery, fantasy, awe, and wonder signify this pre-faith. Children, because they are incapable of comprehending the abstract concept of God, image God through their parents and other significant authority figures' behavior and teachings. These significant people may emphasize God as an ever present, loving Father/Mother/Creator or they may foster the impression that God is a strict taskmaster who keeps a careful record of rights and wrongs and holds them accountable for their actions. The negative images of a stern, manipulative, authority figure, impossible to please, usually translate into fear, worry, and guilt. We carry these early conflicting images into our adult life, although our views may mature during the intervening years. Recently, I heard that one teenager described God rather creatively as a California Highway Patrolman. That could be construed as maturity, perhaps, but I'm not sure what kind!

We experience *literal faith* as school-aged children, who love Bible stories and take them quite literally. Through these colorful stories and further religious training, we get a more consistent and substantial view of God, who, like parents and teachers, rewards good behavior and punishes bad. Rules are very important and disobedience of the commandments — considered sin — is a major cause for concern and guilt. Although sin occurs when we knowingly and purposefully disobey God and hurt others, at the elementary school level, we may often believe mistakes are sin. Children at this age also bargain with God for favors. God is a problem solver or wish fulfiller.

When children enter the teen-age years, they form a strong peer community. Because of peer pressure, they may all state similar beliefs and support each other (peer response) in their religious questions, responses, and challenges. At this stage of *group faith*, young people explore their beliefs as they do their other values with their friends, sometimes playing "follow the leader" in their opposition to their family's cherished religious tradition and practice. They question and even challenge the tenets of their faith, frequently in conjunction with their natural stage of separation from the family unit and movement toward responsible adulthood. These challenges become steppingstones to maturity as they re-evaluate their own relationship with God. Usually at some point later in life — frequently when they marry and/or start a family — those religious values re-surface as they examine their responsibilities to a spouse and children. Eventually, they adjust these values to fit their life experience as well as their family's religious traditions. Life is a process; young people's mistakes, defiance, and relapses into childish behavior happen as they grow through this tumultuous phase of their lives.

When adults begin to question what they believe and why they believe, they are entering into a stage of *personal faith*. It often occurs during a personal crisis, such as a serious illness, a death of a loved one, a divorce, or loss of a job. For others, it happens when the church teachings and authority conflict with this complex twentieth-century world, with its sophisticated media communication, and its phenomenal rapid advancement in all areas of science, including behavioral and biological sciences, medicine, and space. Sometimes one experiences rejection or lack of compassion from a priest or another church authority figure. Others find that the actions of the hierarchical church appear to conflict with the teachings of Jesus, whose primary message is to love God and love and minister to the sinner, the disenfranchised, the lonely, the homeless, the ill, the hungry, and so on. The simple black-and-white answers of the past no longer meet the challenges of the many ethical and human problems of the twentieth and twenty-first centuries.

At this point of differentiation, individuals recognize that the wisdom of their lived experience and their life values have shaped their faith life. They have learned much about themselves and their relationship with God. Their personal faith moves them to stand alone against friends, family, and church authority, if necessary, as they explore the meaning of God at the deepest level. They respond more freely to the call of God, sometimes leaving the church of their childhood to find an expression and celebration of faith elsewhere, one that is more in tune with their relationship with God.

These changes rarely happen overnight. Many years may pass while a person discards the outgrown shell of childhood religion and steps into a new mature personal faith.

Mystical faith is an experience of profound awareness that God dwells within — a sense that one is deeply united with God. This stage is usually marked by the need to live life as meaningfully as possible and to live in communion with one's deep faith values.

Those rare people who reach the stage of *sacrificial faith* — people such as Mother Teresa, Gandhi, and, of course, Jesus — are those whose selfless love and service touches others without regard for their personal safety or needs. These special people willingly sacrifice themselves for the good of others. They exude an aura of quiet holiness, deep compassion, and peace. Many people who are less well known than these great figures also sacrifice themselves every day for the betterment of humanity. They are often found among the poor, the hungry, the homeless, the sick, and the weak. Their commitment becomes their way of life, regardless of where it may lead them, or the risks they may have to face.

Sweeney summarizes the faith journey this way:

> Earlier stages of faith are marked by memorizing, imitation, efforts to please others, and reliance on clear rules and teachings. Later stages of faith are marked by increased honest reflection, ability to examine various points of view, willingness to take responsibility for one's life and decisions, greater service-awareness and commitment to others.

A dear friend and octogenarian, Janet Ward, once shared with us her interesting faith story:

> I was born the daughter of a Methodist deacon. My mother, as part of her ministry, sent barrels of supplies to the Methodist missionaries in China to distribute among the non-Christian poor. Even as an elementary-aged child, I questioned the Christian teaching that excluded those who had not been saved through Jesus Christ by the time of their death. That seemed so cruel to me, especially when a people like the Chinese didn't live in a Christian culture, and probably never had easy access or interest in Christianity. I just couldn't imagine a loving God who would do such a thing!
>
> As I grew up, I questioned all kinds of ministers, priests, and religiously affiliated people. "What happens to those people who die without ever knowing of Jesus?" I'd ask. The standard reply was that all people had to be saved through Jesus Christ.
>
> While I attended Cornell University, I met a member of the Baha'i Faith. His response to that question was, "God is just and loves us all. From the beginning of time, God has sent us teachers and prophets to teach us what we need

to know to have everlasting life. Nobody is neglected or rejected by God." That was like a breath of fresh air to me. It satisfied my longing for a loving God so much that I joined the Baha'i Faith. To this day I continue as an active member and one of my activities is teaching English to Chinese students, whom I love.

As a child, I viewed God as a stern, fearful, benevolent dictator in the sky who saw everything I did and kept a record of my wrongs in a golden book — kind of a grey-bearded Santa Claus "making a list and checking it twice," to see who is naughty and nice. In early Catholic school years, I understood that if I was bad, I was doomed to burn in hell for ever, unless I went to confession — an awesome and fearful experience for a young school child. Everything, it seemed, was sinful. I felt worried and guilty most of the time. I did not think I had much of chance at heaven. I would be lucky to get to purgatory, which really didn't sound all that great either! Some of the positive religious aspects and highlights of that early time for me were prayer, first communion, the processions on high holy days, and the medals, rosaries, prayerbooks, and holy cards I collected for many years.

As a nine-year-old, I remember bargaining with God for snow storms in our rainy winters of northern Oregon. When it did not snow (which was most of the time), I was torn between being angry at God, disbelief in a God who really cares about me, and feeling guilty about my childhood misbehaviors. Yet, remarkably, I was drawn into the mysterious life of faith through prayer.

As I look back, I was a good child, but I didn't get that message. The unconscious tug-of-war between "God's going to get you," and "God loves you" continued until my late twenties with the negative view prevailing. I found it difficult to live with the resulting unrealistic guilt that was constantly reinforced by my two primary teachers, home and church.

In our *Once More With Love* sessions, Catholics in their mid-thirties or older echo those negative images. The rare exception seems to occur when the person lived in a very warm, loving family that demonstrated and mediated for a kinder, gentler God.

For me, *group faith* was similar to *literal faith*. Having been raised in the forties and fifties, neither I nor most of my friends ever really questioned anything. I just accepted and defended my beliefs without question, even though I was aware of some of the inconsistencies in church teaching (for example, that eating a piece of meat on Friday and committing murder had the same value — they were both mortally sinful, and one could go to hell for either one).

I smile now at that corrupted understanding of God as an autocratic, relentless authority, even as I feel the pain of my childhood faith. I feel sad that much of that errant God-view lasted most of my young life. I am amazed that I didn't leave the church, as so many of my friends and family have. Even though my image has matured over the years due to personal growth and education, that earliest image of God still lurks in my consciousness, sometimes nudging me with unnecessary and inappropriate guilt. It has been a difficult task to disconnect from those old negative tapes and to rely on the God of unconditional love and mercy.

When I began teaching religious education in the 1950s, I enrolled in catechist training to prepare to teach. Instructors and other presenters influenced my faith in new ways with continual updating of religious teachings and information. I was excited about what biblical scholarship was beginning to discover. God became less magical, fearful, and distant and became more loveable. As a religious educator, I moved from teaching that sin was a black spot on the white soul and that people "filled up" on grace through sacraments to teaching that sin weakened one's relationship with God, that grace *is* that relationship, that sacraments celebrate the fact that God is uniquely present in peak human experiences, and that one does not have to earn God's love for it is an unconditional free gift. This God was exciting and reachable.

When the Vatican II teachings filtered down through the hierarchy in the late sixties, the fresh air of change began to breeze its way through parish congregations. What a challenge and change! Buried questions rose to the surface as I cautiously left the dark religious closet of my childhood and stepped into the sunlight of an unconditional loving God with my eyes blinking in the brightness.

The trauma of divorce in my late thirties once again challenged my belief in a loving God. When the church, through various individuals, rejected me, I wondered if God condemned me also. During that unsettling time, I had the marvelous opportunity to attend the Seattle University masters of religious education program. In that rarefied air of academia integrated with community, I found healing and promise. I concluded over a period of months that indeed God did not condemn me. God spoke to me in this crisis of compassion, unconditional love, and the healing power of forgiveness. God strengthened me through the unbelievable pain of divorce. My faith transformed, I unwrapped the painful wound of divorce to discover the invaluable gift of new life and a new me.

I began to see the distinct difference between God and the imperfect church. I recognized that the church is a human rather than a divine institution. It does speak for God but often the words get muddled by human frailties and sinfulness. I believe that the Spirit of God is with the church, in spite of some decisions and teachings promulgated in the past that have certainly been less than Godlike. As with each individual, God invites the church — the hierarchical authority and the laity, the people of God — to grow in holiness. God calls the clergy and laity to service, to become the compassionate face of Jesus to the suffering, the disenfranchised, the poor in spirit. Although the church has been dysfunctional at times throughout history, it also has been the vehicle by which great and wonderful things have been done in the name of God. Through the church, we learn of God's unconditional love and Jesus' message of loving service.

Most of us journey through three views of God: God as an autocratic authority, a wish fulfiller, and a friend. Some of us start with no religious upbringing and come late to knowledge of God. Others start with strong religious training through family and church. Others are fortunate to learn about a loving God early in life through loving parental teaching. Still others have to discard early false God images.

Harold S. Kushner in his best seller *When Bad Things Happen to Good People* writes profoundly of a wonderful God "who is the author of all the beauty and order around us, the source of our strength and the hope and courage within us, and of other people's strength and hope and courage with which we are helped in our time of need. We love [God] because he/[she] is the best part of ourselves and of our world."[2] I have read his book several times and I am touched deeply and spiritually by his work.

Our image of God along with our faith stage colors our attitudes and practice of our religion and is key to our spiritual life. It influences how we look at marriage and how we see God in that marital relationship. If we have been raised in a particular religion, we have significant religious values. I have noticed that even non-practicing Catholics make reference to their Catholic background. One reflects a kind of indelible religious identity when one has been raised and educated in a particular faith. Sometimes that early training inhibits the development of a healthy image of God which significantly influences spiritual values and perspectives in life. When these core values clash, substantial stress on the marital relationship occurs. When the individuals share similar views, values, and practice about their understanding of God and their spirituality, stress is reduced while the love and commitment between the spouses is significantly strengthened.

As couples approach a second marriage, they need to explore their attitudes about religion to check for religious conflict. Some attitudes and behaviors are listed below.

♦ Some people separate God and their faith from marriage. They attend church faithfully and follow the church rules, but God is only a Sunday occasion.

♦ Others recognize that they need God to be an integral part of their married life. They expect to practice their faith to the fullest extent by participating in the parish life as much as possible. They take advantage of couples' retreats and other spiritual events that support their marriage. They use all the resources available to them through the church for support. They also pray together and truly call on God to assist them with marital difficulties. They view themselves as partners with God on life's journey.

♦ Some choose the middle ground, attending church regularly and becoming active for occasional parish events, but do not relate to a strong spiritual base.

♦ Still others want to be married in the church to accommodate any social or family pressure. Once they marry, however, they choose to participate only occasionally at liturgy or parish events, if at all.

♦ Some may have been raised in another faith altogether, in which major differences in religious rules and practice are evident and must be taken into consideration.

♦ Others may have had no formal religious training whatso-
ever, and may see no intrinsic value in religion, but they may
not object to their spouse practicing a particular religion as
long as they do not have to get involved.

♦ Some persons live a very rich, internal spiritual life, but
speak sparingly of their personal spirituality.

♦ Some persons are rigid and unbending in their beliefs, others
are open and flexible.

When we accept God as a partner in the relationship we
commit ourselves to working together from a "God point-of-view."
In other words, once we make the decision that we want to live
a life of love and commitment with another in the sacrament of
marriage, we accept that person as he or she is without expectation
of change; then we make every effort to love our partner without
condition just as God loves us.

A God point-of-view includes forgiveness, acceptance, vul-
nerability, and risk. We willingly tap into God's strength in each of
us — that sacramental grace — to work through crises and resolve
problems creatively. When we get into a bind of anger or hurt we
ask God in prayer to help us re-open the door of communication,
as well as opening our minds and hearts so that we may listen to
each other's perspective from a God point-of-view. After hearing
each other out, we may ask ourselves "What is God's way, the most
loving and appropriate action, we can take in this situation?"

Most of the time couples do well. Only when we put ourselves
in charge during tough times do we sometimes block our openness
to the God point-of-view. The trick is for both persons to be willing
to trust each other as they work out the most loving, responsible,
and appropriate response to a situation. Cooperating with God and
each other by using God as our source of love and power can indeed
enrich our relationship.

The Sacrament of Christian Marriage

The sacrament of Christian marriage is a sacred celebration
of the sign of God's presence in the permanent loving union and
faithful commitment of two Christian people in marriage. The
bride and groom make mutual, unconditional promises to love and

cherish one another for life. In this risky and rich commitment, the couple trust that God will grace them with loving strength through difficult times. They affirm that the healing power of God's love will cast out fear of failure and replace it with trust in each other. They also ask their witnesses — family, friends, and the Christian community represented by a priest or minister — to support them in Christian love and celebrate this joyous occasion with them.

Prior to the renewal of the Second Vatican Council, the word contract was often used to describe the union of marriage. Following the council, the church began to enrich this notion with the image of a covenant. Like the bond between God and his people, the union of marriage is a covenant of love and fidelity between two persons. The love of the couple, exemplifies the sustaining, faithful love that God has for all people. Sacramental marriage also reflects the union between Christ and the church.

The sacramental graces bestowed upon the Christian couple on their wedding day are lifetime blessings. The power and presence of the sacrament continue as the spirit of Jesus Christ sustains them in their pain and dances with them in their joy. Couples who live in love, fidelity, growth, and service witness to the power and presence of Christ in their lives.

Marriage is not static. In "The Sacrament of Marriage," a *Catholic Update* article written by Mary and James Kenny, the authors state: ". . . [marriage] is an intimate partnership in which each person gives the other freedom to grow. . . ." Mutual growth promotes the individual development of each partner and includes good communication skills, open expression of feelings, balance between assertiveness and surrender, positive outlook regarding one's partner, marriage renewal and enrichment, and trust in the love that the couple shares, even when dry spells occur. The Kennys write the following about total commitment:

> Total commitment enables Christian marriage partners to say to each other: "You will grow and change, and so will I. We know that; we expect it. Growth and change are not things to fear but are part of the adventure that is our life together. If growth leads you to success in paths I cannot follow, I will rejoice in your victory. If change means loss of health or disappointment, I will still be there. If change brings differences between us, we shall work them out. You do not have to be afraid to grow. You do not have to fear

what growth will do to our marriage. Before all else, we are committed to working out our life together."[3]

There are no guarantees to the successful lifelong commitment of Christian marriage. Life twists and turns unexpectedly. Marriage is an open-ended, unconditional promise to love "for better, for worse, for richer, for poorer . . . until death do us part." Many couples who enter a second marriage understand more completely the true meaning of that kind of love, particularly after the failure of a previous marriage. Second-timers do not enter into this commitment lightly. Most do, however, enter Christian marriage trusting that God will sustain them with the sacramental graces needed to remain faithful to their wedding vows.

Updating Our Faith

Some couples who attend *Once More With Love* have not updated their religious education since their school years. Some have felt alienated from church due to a previous religious or marriage problem. Others feel betrayed by the confusing and sometimes misunderstood changes of the Second Vatican Council. Some are amazingly unaware of the Vatican II changes altogether. Vatican II, new developments in theology, and advances in scripture scholarship during the past forty years or so have promoted new and rich insights into Catholic teachings and practice. Some problems of the past are resolvable today, especially marriage problems. It behooves one to speak to a gentle priest who is in tune with the church's current practice to discover one's standing in today's church. Many inactive Catholics sincerely desire to be accepted by the church as members in good standing and to practice their faith once again. I believe that a pleasant surprise awaits those who investigate their situation further.

In a recent parish bulletin, a flyer was enclosed stating:

THE CATHOLIC CHURCH WANTS TO MAKE A CONFESSION. We wanted to share love, to worship God the Father, Son and Holy Spirit. We wanted the whole world to believe in Jesus and follow God's commandments. But sometimes, instead of touching you, we pushed too hard. When you needed someone to listen, we offered a reprimand, and when you questioned, we turned you away.

> If somehow we've hurt you, please know that we're sorry. And if you can find forgiveness in your heart, please give us another chance.
> _____Catholic Church. . . extends a warm invitation to non-practicing or inactive Catholics to take another look at the church through a process of hearing your stories, answering questions, and providing information on current church beliefs and practices.
> Our series is on _____. You are invited to any or all of the six sessions. There is no registration. For more information, call _____.

This style of invitation is showing up in parishes all over the country. It is a badly needed apology to those who have been rejected, angered, and hurt by past experiences with the Catholic church. Non-practicing Catholics welcome this warm invitation to return for information in an atmosphere of freedom and reconciliation. This particular parish had seventy attendees the first night!

Today, new understandings of church teachings and practices motivate Catholics to explore adult religious education. Maybe some of the brief sketches below will encourage further exploration.

God

God is the total masculine and feminine principle. God is Father and Mother and Creator. She is the essence of life who set the universe and our heartbeat in motion. He loves us unconditionally. Nothing we have ever done, or will ever do, can stop her from loving us. Like a loving parent, God invites us to return her love by taking one step at a time toward wholeness, and by respect and care for each other. Though we may stumble and fall, he reaches out to help us up and gently holds our hand as we proceed forward. God is all-encompassing and beyond description. No religion has the total picture of this loving Power that dwells within us yet transcends the universe. Each religion contributes a piece of understanding to the picture, but when we put it all together, we still cannot truly comprehend God.

God's Will

God does not necessarily tap someone on the shoulder to say that he or she should be a doctor, writer, plumber, priest or sister.

God wills that each of us be happy in this world and in the next.
Whatever we choose to do in life, as long as we follow God's law
of love and respect toward others rather than focusing only on our
own selfishness and disregard for others, is God's will. Our faith
response is to become our most authentic self.

Prayer

Prayer for me is when I retreat to the deepest part of me —
my soul and conscience — and stand before God. It is the place
where I am true to myself, for I cannot fake it before God. God
created me and knows me more intimately than I know myself.
"I can never forget you! I have written your name on the palms
of my hands" (Is 49:15). In that loving presence, I tap into God's
power within, state my case, or listen in the quiet stillness for the
loving response of God. Prayer expresses our deeply held values
and attitudes about life and God. God does not need our prayer,
we do. Prayer changes our heart and helps us focus on the God
point-of-view throughout our lives.

The Bible

The Bible is a special work of literature that describes and
interprets a people's relationship with God. The Bible is composed
of Hebrew scriptures — the religious history of the Israelites — and
Christian scriptures — the story of Jesus Christ and the development of the Christian church. Folklore, legal documents, sermons,
prayer songs, poetry, proverbs, narratives and parables are some of
the various types of writing found within its covers. We believe
that all the writers of the scriptures, both Jewish and Christian,
were inspired to record their unique faith journey with God. Jesus
and his followers were Jews. Therefore, the roots of the Christian
story are found in the Hebrew scriptures.

Jesus in the Gospels

Virginia Smith, in her Catholic Update article "The Four Faces
of Jesus," describes Jesus as a many faceted character.[4] The earliest
and shortest gospel of Mark was written for Roman followers of

Jesus. It opens with Jesus' baptism by John the Baptist and describes an earthy, human, compassionate Jesus, always on the go with crowds following closely in his footsteps. He teaches through action. No one ever approaches Jesus without being healed in mind, body, or spirit.

Writing for the Jews in bustling Antioch in Syria, a hub of activity in the early Christian world, Matthew's Jesus is the promised Messiah. Matthew opens his gospel by tracing Jesus' lineage back to well-known heroes and prophets of the Hebrew scriptures, especially identifying him as the new Moses. One of the infancy narratives, which includes the three kings and the flight to Egypt stories, begins Jesus' life. Matthew draws parallels between Moses and Jesus, while highlighting him as the Messiah. For instance, Moses goes to the mountain to speak to God, while Jesus teaches from the mountain to show his own authority. One of the five major discourses found in Matthew is the Sermon on the Mount.

Luke, a Greek convert, writes to gentiles like himself living in southern Greece. Luke's gospel also opens with an infancy narrative similar to Matthew's, but it includes the angel's announcement to Mary that she will give birth to the Son of God and the shepherds' visit to the manger. Luke portrays Jesus as a gentle, loving, forgiving person. In this gospel, the Holy Spirit is referred to frequently and women have a prominent role. Jesus teaches about universal salvation available to everyone. He shows great compassion for the fringe people of his community, the public sinners, the poor, and the sick. The Good Samaritan and the Prodigal Son stories are found only in the gospel of Luke. Scripture scholars believe that Luke also wrote the Acts of the Apostles, the book that follows the gospels.

John's gospel, written years later, is much more theologically developed. John describes Jesus as noble, domestic, divine. "Whoever has seen me has seen the Father" (Jn 14:9). Jesus is always in control, and knows everything that will happen to him.

Virginia Smith concludes her article by writing: "All Christians are called to portray the face of Jesus in their own lives, to be living gospels: facets of the great prism through which the light of Christ shines out to a waiting world."

Sunday Liturgy

A "support group" of Christians, the people of God, the Christian community, the body of Christ — all describe those who come together to bless, break open the word of God, the Christian story, and share the body of Christ, the Son of God, our savior and guide. We focus on Jesus, who leads us to our Creator God and shows us how to live a life of service and love in response to God's call. Frequent participation in Sunday services helps us stay in touch with our Christian power base, not always validated in our daily world. We also come to this weekly service — the Christian community's public worship of God through Jesus — to celebrate Jesus' life, death and resurrection by taking and eating the body and blood of Christ in the elements of bread and wine.

Sacraments

The Catholic church is a sacramental church in which the people of God liturgically celebrate major life events by highlighting the fact that God is present in these human events as in all of life.

♦ We celebrate birth and new life through the sacrament of *baptism*, an invitation and celebration of the child entering the Christian community through his or her parents. Adults enter the Catholic Christian community through the Rite of Christian Initiation of Adults (RCIA). This process follows the pattern of the early church — providing extensive preparation and faith sharing in specific stages for initiation into the Christian community at the Easter Vigil. The one-to-three year journey concludes with celebration of the sacraments of baptism, confirmation, and eucharist.

♦ In the sacrament of *confirmation*, we celebrate and affirm our membership in the Christian family and confirm the implicit belief that God showers us with an unconditional, forgiving love. We acknowledge that the gifts of the Holy Spirit strengthen us in all the seasons of our life.

♦ We celebrate the sacrament of *eucharist*, the Christian family meal, in which Jesus — the sacrament of God — becomes the food for our life journey under the forms of bread and wine. We gather at this special meal to remember our family story of Jesus and our loving God, to reconcile with those from whom we feel alienated, and to eat together as the sign and source of our family unity.

♦ We celebrate the sacrament of *reconciliation* when we accept God's eternal mercy and forgiveness for our wrongdoing. Our reconciliation with God and with those in the Christian community whom we have hurt heals our spirit and reunites us all in Christian love.

♦ We celebrate the sacrament of *marriage*, the public consent to live a life of love and commitment with one person exclusively. This bond that brings forth new life in love reflects the love that God has for all creation, and the incredible power of love to heal, transform, and unify.

♦ We celebrate the sacrament of *holy orders*, through which a man is ordained to serve the church as a deacon, priest, or bishop. The man commits himself to a life of compassionate, caring ministry to others in the name of God, and takes on the responsibility of becoming the official presider at liturgical and sacramental celebrations.

♦ We celebrate physical and emotional healing through the sacrament of the *anointing of the sick*. With blessed oil as an ancient sign of power and strength, we affirm God's healing power over mind, body, and spirit.

Life is a journey of faith for Christians. We are either moving toward God or away from God. In our workshops, many of our participants have received an early impression of a negative, harsh, manipulative God. However, through their life journey, they have discovered a loving, faithful friend in God.

Occasionally participants have been badly scarred religiously and are harboring guilt and bitterness toward the church. Sometimes, our workshop on religious values is the first positive experience a participant has had about God and religion in a long time. Arthur expresses this sentiment on his evaluation form at the end of one of our sessions:

This class was the one I dreaded the most. I had, by choice, been away from the church for many years. Tonight's class

160 ONCE MORE WITH LOVE

has started to open my eyes as to the new teaching of the
Catholic church. Maybe I can feel comfortable for the first
time in my life with the religion that I thought was lost to
me forever. Maybe I am not such a bad guy after all?

Another time, an older gentleman attended our class the first
night and pulled me aside at the break. He indicated that the
reason he came was to find out his status in the church. Tense
and upset, he believed he was excommunicated from the church
because of a divorce fifteen years before. He had not been to church
or the sacraments in many years. After the class, we spent an hour
with him listening to his heart-rending story and giving him some
updated information on the church. Most of all, he needed to know
that God loved him, and that the information he received from
a priest following the divorce was incorrect. We told him that he
did indeed have a place in the church. Then, we referred him
to a very compassionate priest for further spiritual direction. The
relief and gratitude he felt showed in his tearful eyes. He said as
he went out the door, "I want to make peace with my church and
I want to receive communion." He gratefully finished the Once
More With Love sessions and was married in the church within a
few months.

Occasionally, we receive criticism from Catholics for offering
remarriage classes for Catholics or including Catholic participants
who do not have an annulment. One woman asked, "Aren't you
promoting remarriage outside the church by helping couples to
make a better marriage?" The following is our response.

Once More With Love is designed to offer information, awareness, and preparation for the special concerns of second marriages.
We certainly focus on the Catholic perspective of permanence,
because we truly believe in it. However, our participants make
their own decisions. Most couples, already in marriage preparation,
are referred to our program by a priest. Some have annulments
or are in the process; others come without such a referral and do
not have an annulment. We never close the door on them, for
we believe our program stands on its own merits and reputation
as valuable for anyone considering second marriage. We frequently
feel God working through us, gently inviting non-practicing Catholics toward re-entry into the church.

There remains a great deal of misinformation about the church and its teachings, particularly around the issues of marriage, divorce, remarriage, and annulments. We provide a forum in which some of it can be corrected, as demonstrated in the above-mentioned cases. Some Catholics who enter our program feel that the church has closed the door on them. We open the door and say, "Welcome. How can we help you?"

Since Catholics have a poor understanding of annulments (see "Annulment Is Not Catholic Divorce" below), we spend some time discussing that subject. Some couples really want to have their marriages blessed in the church, and they welcome the updated information we can provide. We have had several couples start annulment proceedings following our classes. Without our program, they may never have done so.

We became close friends of another couple who joined one of our classes. They were waiting to set their wedding date as soon as the annulment papers came through. After fifteen months, the papers still had not been processed through the first judgment, even though all necessary and appropriate forms had been submitted within the first thirty days. Marilee states:

> Ken and I decided to marry before a civil judge, rather than live together, after we felt that we had waited a reasonable time for the declaration of nullity to be processed. When the papers did arrive a few months later, our work schedules did not permit us to begin formal preparations for the sacramental blessing of the church, so we delayed it. We had a home mass and renewed our wedding promises instead.
>
> On our first anniversary, we were having some step-parenting difficulties and chose to delay the formal ceremony again, until we were in a better place. We did have our rings blessed and celebrated our anniversary in the context of another home mass.
>
> On our second anniversary we were ready for the formal sacramental blessing and a small celebration with family and friends.
>
> We believe we were married in the eyes of God from the moment of the civil ceremony. At no time did we feel we were "living in sin." We continued to attend our parish liturgies, participate in parish activities, and receive the sacraments. God continued to grace our lives with his

love. Our prayerful decisions about this most important event, the spiritual direction from our priest, and the power of God in our union gave us the strength to make the appropriate response for our particular situation. We have never regretted it.

Any divorce or failed marriage, whether valid in the eyes of the church or not, injures the whole institution of marriage. We help couples prepare for the particular concerns of second marriage so that the incidence of divorce is reduced. We wish to encourage, stimulate, strengthen, and enhance healthy married family life.

I received a letter from a friend living at some distance from us who remarried in the church after receiving a declaration of nullity. She and her fiance did not attend second marriage preparation. She wrote:

> I knew my second husband for ten years, and was married to him for only three months before I left; but obviously, I never left the dating stage. If I had had the opportunity to take your course, I'm sure there would never have been a marriage. When I did ask a priest if there was such a course, he said to me, "You've been married before. I don't think you need that at your age!"

Annulment Is Not Catholic Divorce

Today, approximately one out of two marriages end in divorce. Although Catholics believe in one indissoluble marriage for life, Catholic marriages fail at about the same rate as non-Catholic marriages. After a civil divorce, Catholics may petition for a church annulment. Because there are many misconceptions and myths that pervade the Catholic population's understanding of annulment, less than ten percent of divorced Catholics have ever petitioned for one.

We want to correct any annulment misinformation and dispel some of the mystery regarding annulments so that divorced Catholics can better determine whether they would like to present their case to their diocesan marriage tribunal for review.

Some of the annulment myths and misunderstandings are:

◆ A divorced Catholic is excommunicated from the church.

◆ A divorced Catholic does not believe in indissolubility of marriage.

♦ An annulment is a Catholic divorce.

♦ One cannot get an annulment if the marriage was a long one.

♦ Annulment means that any children born of the marriage are illegitimate.

♦ An annulment takes years to process.

♦ Annulments are very expensive.

♦ The decision for annulment depends on whether you can pay or not.

♦ Annulment means we were illegally married.

We will answer each of these statements and give further general information about church annulments.

Excommunication

A divorced Catholic is never excommunicated from the church and may participate fully in the church's sacramental life, including reception of the eucharist. This is validated through Pope John Paul II's *Apostolic Exhortation on the Family*:

> Together with the synod, I earnestly call upon pastors and the whole community of the faithful to help the divorced and with solicitous care to make sure that they do not consider themselves as separated from the church, for as baptized persons they can and indeed must share in her life . . . (*Familiaris Consortio*, 1987).

Annulment

Jeffrey Keefe, O.F.M., Conv., in his article "Why the Church Is Granting More Annulments," defines an annulment (or "declaration of nullity" as it is more properly named):

> A declaration of nullity is a judgment by the Church (through the Diocesan Tribunal) that what seemed to be a marriage never was in fact a true marriage. An annulment is not a divorce for it does not dissolve an existing marriage. A declaration of nullity is granted when it can be shown that some essential or juridical defect made a particular marriage invalid from the beginning despite outward appearance, despite even the good faith of the partners or the establishment of a family.[5]

In other words, the church tribunal reviews a marriage and judges whether a valid sacramental marriage existed from the beginning. An annulment declares that there was not such a sacramental bond, despite any appearances to the contrary. Annulments are not difficult to obtain given the streamlined procedures of the church's *Code of Canon Law* and the expanded psychological grounds for nullity. In the last twenty years, there has been an explosion of petitions for annulments and today, nine out of ten petitioners who complete the process receive a declaration of nullity. We will not cover specific grounds for annulment here. Couples or individuals can contact their diocesan tribunal office to obtain further information about grounds. Excellent information on grounds can be found in the book *Annulment: Do You Have a Case?* by Terence E. Tierney, J.C.L.[6]

It is important to note here that the law of the United States permits priests or ministers to marry couples civilly as well as religiously, as long as the people involved are following the tenets of that religion. Therefore, since a couple was civilly married, they must obtain a civil divorce before applying for a church annulment. In Europe, the civil laws require a separate civil marriage ceremony. You may have heard of weddings in Europe where the couple has two ceremonies, one before a civil official, then a religious ceremony before their priest or minister.

Children and the Duration of Marriage

Because the declaration of nullity judges only the validity of the Catholic marriage according to canon law, any children of the marriage are never considered illegitimate. Also, the length of the marriage does not affect the validity since the determination of nullity is based on grounds present at the beginning of the marriage. The judgment is not to lay blame on one or the other partner. It only states whether the marriage itself was valid or invalid at the beginning according to church law.

Petitions

Any divorced person, Catholic or not, may present a marriage case to the diocesan tribunal. In fact, many non-Catholics petition the church for a declaration of nullity, especially if they plan to marry a Catholic. The person who initiates the petition is called the petitioner. Their former partner is named the respondent, whether he or she participates or not. It is not necessary that the respondent reply or even participate in order for the process to continue. However, the procedure may be delayed without his or her cooperation. The respondent will be notified that a petition for annulment is in process and the grounds on which it is based. He or she will then be given time to respond. Likewise, at the end of the process, a copy of the declaration of nullity or the denial is sent to the petitioner and respondent. The petitions, witness statements, and proceedings are always kept strictly confidential.

Time of Process

The diocese of San Jose, California can serve as an example of the time involved. It takes between six and eighteen months to process and judge a case. The time depends on how long it takes to gather and process the required papers, interview former spouses and witnesses, conduct the investigation of the evidence, and present, review, and judge the case. The variance in time is determined by how quickly required papers, witness statements, and responses are returned, or if there is a backload of cases to be handled, or if there is lack of clerical help to do the paper work. Some cases can be processed quickly due to an easily documented legal defect in the procedure of the marriage, while more complicated cases take more time.

The Tribunal

A marriage tribunal exists in every diocese. It consists of the judicial vicar (the presiding judge and administrator representing the bishop), at least two judges (who hear the cases and render judgments), the defender of the bond (who protects the rights of both parties and argues as far as possible for the validity of the marital bond), advocates (who assist the petitioner and the respondent through the process), and clerical assistants. The judicial vicar, judges, defender of the bond, and advocates are usually priests, religious, or lay persons appropriately trained and experienced in canon law.

This diocesan tribunal is also called the court of the first instance, where petitions are begun and a decision or judgment is made. Since 1983, canon law requires that any petitions granted in a court of the first instance must be reviewed by a court of the second instance. In California, the tribunal of the archdiocese of San Francisco is the regional court of the second instance for the bay area dioceses. The purpose of the second court is to examine the work and decision of the first court to insure correct procedures were followed and the judgment was appropriate. This mandatory procedure adds four to six weeks time to complete the annulment process.

Costs

Costs vary from diocese to diocese. In the San Jose diocese the fee is $350 for costs of time spent for clerical help, investigation, and presentation of the case. This actually accounts for about one-third of the cost of handling a marriage case. The fee may be paid with the petition, in some form of extended payment plan, or waived for those who are unable to pay. Payment or non-payment does not influence the judgment of the case. Those who judge the case do not know whether the petitioner has paid fees or not.

The Process

To begin the process, a person sets an appointment with either a knowledgeable parish priest or a diocesan tribunal staff person. At this initial appointment the discussion will focus on the past marital history and possible grounds for annulment. If a person gets a negative response from the priest, he or she should get a second opinion by setting an appointment with someone at the tribunal office. They are better trained to evaluate a marriage and may see grounds that a parish priest may have overlooked.

At that first interview, the petitioner will be required to fill out some forms, and will be given a questionnaire to complete at home which is a guide for the petitioner to write in his or her own words a history of the courtship, marriage, and break-up. The petitioner must send in certified copies of documents such as baptismal, marriage, and divorce records, along with the completed questionnaire and the names and addresses of witnesses and the former spouse.

Witnesses usually will be asked about the personalities of the couple involved in the marriage. They do not need to be experts, simply people who knew the husband and wife. The best witnesses are neutral people, that is, friends of both partners, but other witnesses will be considered if necessary.

Once the initial paperwork has been completed and returned to the tribunal, the case is given a number. This signals that the petition has been formally accepted. The respondent is notified of the petition and is invited to respond. Some respondents are uncooperative or are not interested in participating in the process. Their lack of cooperation usually does not halt the process.

The tribunal gathers information from the petitioner, respondent, and witnesses through written documents and interviews and prepares the case for a hearing. Sometimes a psychologist's written testimony is required as an expert witness in the matter. Occasionally, the petitioner may be interviewed a second time. If the advocate needs any further information or has anything to report, he or she will contact the petitioner. During the waiting period, the petitioner can call his or her advocate at any time to check on the progress of the case.

When all the information is complete and the case is prepared, it is handed on to the judges for study and a hearing. Usually the petitioner and witnesses do not attend this hearing. The positions are presented in writing and orally before the judges. The hearing is recorded and later transcribed and placed in a confidential file. The judges' decision comes in written form and is sent on to the court of the second instance for review. Within three or four weeks it is returned to the court of the first instance, usually with approval, and a copy of the declaration of nullity is sent to the petitioner and the respondent. Should the petition be denied, either party may appeal to the court of second instance (an appellate court).

Benefits

Although the annulment process is long, sometimes painful, and difficult for the petitioner who sorts out his or her personal history of the marriage, many Catholics speak of the value of this experience. They find that completing this process brings healing, peace, and closure to very painful memories. It becomes a steppingstone that allows them to let go of the past and open to a new beginning. Even those who wait many years to apply for an annulment find it cathartic. It often affirms one's belief that the marriage never reflected God's unconditional love and forgiveness at all. Some comment on the new insights about themselves and marriage that they discovered. Others recognize the gifts that emerged from the tragedy of the broken marriage. Still others find the experience provides good background and preparation for a second marriage.

The additional benefit that most Catholics speak of is the right to marry again with the church's blessing. For those who have remarried, before an annulment of a first marriage is declared, it offers them the opportunity to return to the eucharistic table of the Lord.

Internal Forum

Remarried Catholics who, for one reason or another, are unable to obtain an annulment (the external forum), may seek counsel with their spiritual advisor regarding an internal forum solution (sometimes referred to as a "good conscience" solution). For instance, if a person believes that the former marriage was invalid, but cannot prove an annulment case, he or she may privately consult with a priest or spiritual advisor familiar with this personal approach.

The consultant cannot give permission to receive sacraments, but he or she can assist an individual or a couple to examine their responsibility toward the past failed marriage and provide counsel as they clarify their present relationship with God. With the help of prayer and a caring advisor, the individual or the couple make their own conscience decision regarding reception of the sacraments.

Eucharist is a sign and source of unity in and with the church. It is not meant to be a "gold star" for obedience. Those who choose to receive eucharist do so out of deep desire to participate in this sacrament as the sustenance — Jesus — that feeds them on their journey of faith and provides support for fidelity to each other and the church.

The internal forum is a conscience approach and is not governed by the public law of the church. It is a private affair similar to confession and should remain so. Once the decision is made, the couple need not report it to anyone else, including another priest. Couples who do receive sacraments in good conscience without benefit of annulment may want to attend another parish if their approach to the sacraments causes scandal. For further information, contact your spiritual advisor or a priest familiar and comfortable with this approach.

Additional Notes

♦ The tribunal personnel always welcome appointments with anyone to answer questions about the annulment process. One may make an appointment for information or counseling without committing oneself to the annulment process.

♦ At any time, the petitioner can request that the process be halted until he or she is ready to continue.

♦ It is advised, although not required, that a petition for annulment be initiated at least a year after the civil divorce, so that a more objective view of the marriage is presented.

♦ Remarried Catholics who have not received an annulment are not excommunicated from the church. According to canon law, however, they may not receive eucharist.

♦ Because the Catholic church recognizes the validity of marriages of all Christian denominations, a divorced non-Catholic preparing to marry a Catholic may need to petition the tribunal for an annulment. Because this is a complex issue, contact your tribunal for clarification.

Conclusion

Remarriage offers couples a new opportunity to grow and be enriched through a loving, lifelong relationship. However, even the most flexible and tolerant people are challenged by the enormous complexities in remarriage. Individuals must be willing to work at the relationship, using their best communication and negotiating skills while developing their spiritual power through prayer. God's incredible love for us truly empowers us to overcome even very difficult situations.

If you sense early on that walls are forming between you and your spouse, seek professional help. The right counselor can assist you to sort out and clarify the issues and facilitate your discovery of new, acceptable ways of relating to each other. Reinforce your spiritual base by upgrading your religious education through occasional workshops and parish programs. Couple retreats, Marriage Encounter, and spiritual direction can also support your relationship. Use these opportunities to build your couple strength. Energize the power of God within you through prayer. Do not permit walls to develop that will divide you. Hang in there, keep talking, and protect your relationship with an abundance of loving care. We wish you happiness and a long life of love together.

> Then I saw a new heaven and a new earth.
> The first heaven and the first earth disappeared,
> and the sea vanished. . .
> I heard a loud voice speaking from the throne:
> "Now God's home is with all people.
> God will live with them
> and they shall be God's people
> and God shall be their God
> who is always with them.
> God will wipe away all tears from their eyes.
> There will be no more death, no more grief
> or crying or pain. The old things have disappeared.
> . . .And now I make all things new!"
>
> — *adapted from Revelation 21:1–5*

Religion
WORKSHEET

Privately answer the questions, or respond to the statements with *Agree* or *Disagree*. Then share with your partner.

1. Name five beliefs you have about God.

2. As a child, my image of God was...
   Today, I believe God is like...

3. I believe in God because...

4. I believe God loves me unconditionally regardless of my past or future failures.

5. There is nothing I have ever done or will ever do that will stop God from loving me.

6. We discuss religious issues and our relationship with God with each other.

7. Our faith in Jesus Christ makes/will make our marriage Christian.

8. My religious preference has caused some conflict with my partner.

9. My partner's attachment to his/her church is a problem for me.

10. Some areas of possible conflict regarding faith and church issues are...

11. I have difficulty practicing some of the teachings of my church.

12. One aspect of church I would like to discuss or have clarified is...

13. One aspect I especially appreciate is...

14. An aspect of church I disagree with is...

15. My partner is comfortable with the way I follow the teachings of my church.

16. My faith strongly influences the way I live my life.

17. Prayer is very important to me.

18. My partner and I sometimes pray together.

19. The kind of things I pray about are . . .

20. I believe my partner's faith influences his/her life a great deal.

21. I have difficulty sharing my faith and religious values with my partner.

22. It is important to me that there is a religious dimension to our relationship.

23. It is important to me that my partner and I share religious preference.

24. I want my children to follow my religious preference.

25. One good religious experience I have had is . . .

26. One bad religious experience I have had is . . .

27. Regular participation in mass and communion is necessary to my faith.

28. An important part of my religious commitment is to reach out to others.

29. On a scale of 1–10, how religious am I? My partner?

30. I want to be married in the Catholic church because . . .

31. I understand the meaning of marriage as sacrament.

32. The difference between a sacramental and non-sacramental marriage is . . .

33. We have been in contact with a priest regarding our wedding.

34. I want us to plan our wedding ceremony, including our pledges to each other.

35. It is a necessary part of my Christian commitment to be active in my parish.

36. We both agree about the amount of involvement we wish to have in our church.

37. I have an annulment.

38. I want more information on annulments.

39. We agree that marriage commits us to Christ and binds us together for life.

40. Unconditional love and commitment are necessary for a lifelong relationship.

41. I believe marriage requires work and prayer.

42. I expect to continue my personal growth and individuality after marriage.

43. I would like us to go on an occasional couple retreat after we are married.

44. I will stand by and support my spouse in difficult times as well as happy times.

45. I will rejoice in my spouse's personal growth and will work with him/her to resolve any problems that this growth entails.

46. I recognize there may be some dry times in our marriage.

47. I believe Christian marriage is an intimate partnership in which each person gives the other freedom to grow.

48. Fidelity in marriage is commitment to grow as a couple in mutual support and love.

49. I am committed to learn how to work out our individual differences with each other.

50. I believe our differences will enrich us.

51. I want us to focus on the positive, loving qualities that brought us together.

52. I want our home to be an open, loving, and hospitable place for family and friends.

53. The church can be helpful to us in the following ways . . .

54. Write a personal statement of your religious beliefs.

Additional Notes:

Statement of Faith

We believe in God, in Jesus Christ, in the Holy Spirit, and in you and in me.

We believe the Holy Spirit has freed us to worship as a community.

We believe the Holy Spirit works through
balloons and ministers
daisies and wiggly children
clanging cymbals and silence
drama and the unexpected
choirs and banners
touching and praying
spontaneity and planning
faith and doubt
tears and laughter
leading and supporting
hugging and kneeling
dancing and stillness
applauding and giving
creativity and plodding
words and listening
holding and letting go
thank you and help me
Scripture and alleluias
agonizing and celebrating
accepting and caring
through you and through me
through Love.

We believe God's Holy Spirit lives in this community of dancing, hand-holding people where lines of age and politics and life- styles are crossed.

We believe in praising God for Life.

We believe in responding to God's grace and love and justice for all people.

We believe in the poetry within each of us.

We believe in dreams and visions.

We believe in old people running and children leading.

We believe in the Kingdom of God within us.

We believe in Love.[7]

— Ann Weems
Reaching For Rainbows

Summary

Unfinished Business

Have you made peace with the past marriage failure? Have you let go of the bitterness, anger, and unrealistic guilt? Are you now living in the present and looking toward the future? Have you completed all unfinished business of the past: divorce, annulment? Are you maintaining your legal and moral responsibilities to your past family? Do you feel you have reached a measure of adult autonomy, a sense of confidence and self-esteem? Do you feel free to choose not to remarry and still be happy?

Acceptance

Do you have a real friendship with your present partner? Have you looked honestly and objectivly at your partner, seeing his/her faults, limitations and idiosyncrasies? Are you willing to spend your life with this person without changes? Do you feel your partner accepts you as you are in the same way? Do you truly love each other and accept each other?

Communication

Do you listen with heart and mind to your partner's feelings and share your own feelings? Are you able to ask for you what you want and need and accept only what can be given? Are you open, flexible, willing, and commited to resolving problems through creative negotiation rather than trying to win the argument? Are you willing to apologize when you are wrong and forgive and forget when your partner is wrong? Are you willing to accept the best solutions for the situation rather than be right? Will you continue to use the worksheets and similar feeling questions to maintain open communication? Are you willing to seek outside help with problems if it becomes necessary? Are you willing to work together to build a lifelong relationship, resolving problems rather than ignoring them or quitting the relationship? Do you need more time to prepare for this marriage?

Values

Are your values similar enough that there will be shared understanding and decision-making on important issues such as finances, children, and religious issues? Will you allow time and be patient as you begin to work out your life together? Are you willing to support your partner in his/her growth?

Children

Are you prepared to take time to bond with your stepchildren rather than pushing for love and acceptance immediately? Are you prepared to deal with possible problems either with the stepchildren or former spouses? Are you open to the creation of a new family and willing to seek professional help to better prepare for the blending of this new family?

Finances

Have you shared your financial assets and liabilities in order to plan for your future? Are you prepared to accept financial responsibility for each other and any stepchildren? Have you made plans about where you will live and how you will blend your personal belongings?

Intimacy and Religion

Do you truly share love between you enough to make a commitment for life? Do you each believe and act as if your relationship is primary over all other persons and things? Do you recognize the presence of God as an integral part of your relationship with each other? Accepting God in your relationship, are you willing to witness his love for you in your love for each other, and witness that love to your families, friends and community? Will you regularly plan fresh quality time alone with your partner to enhance your loving relationship?

Why do you want to get married?

What is the greatest gift you bring to your relationship?

What is the greatest gift your partner brings to your relationship?

Apache Wedding Blessing

Now there is no lonliness for you.
Now you will feel no rain,
For each of you will be shelter to the other.
Now you will feel no cold,
For each of you will be warmth to the other.
Now there is no loneliness for you,
Now there is no more loneliness.
Now you are two persons but there is one life before you.
Go now to your dwelling place
To enter into the days of your togetherness.
And may your days be good and long upon the earth.

References and Resources

Chapter 1

1. Robert S. Weiss, *Marital Separation* (New York: Basic Books, Inc., 1975), p. 46.

2. North American Conference of Separated and Divorced Catholics, Inc. Central Office: 1100 S. Goodman St., Rochester, NY 14620; (716) 271-1320.

3. Ken and Becky Eggeman, "Emotional Growth in Marriage," *Marriage and Family Living* (April 1979), p. 5.

4. Maury Smith O.F.M., D. Min., *A Practical Guide to Value Clarification*, University Associates, Inc., La Jolla, CA, 1977. This checklist was originally expressed by Louis E. Raths, Merrill Harmin, and Sidney B. Simon.

5. David Keirsey and Marilyn Bates, *Please Understand Me — Character and Temperament Types* (Del Mar, CA: Prometheus Nemesis Books, 1978).

6. Maria Beesing, O.P., Robert J. Nogosek, C.S.C., and Patrick H. O'Leary, S.J., *The Enneagram — A Journey of Self Discovery* (Danville, NJ: Dimension Books, Inc., 1984).

7. Richard Rohr and Andreas Ebert, *Discovering the Enneagram — An Ancient Tool for a New Spiritual Journey* (New York: Crossroad Publishing Company, 1990).

Chapter 2

1. James Greteman, CSC, *Coping With Divorce* (Notre Dame, IN: Ave Maria Press, 1981) p. 28.

2. James Tunstead Burtchaell, CSC, "An Ancient Gift, A Thing of Joy," *Notre Dame Magazine* (Winter 1985/86, Vol. 14, No. 4), p. 15.

3. Barb Upham, "Love." Copyright © 1986, Blue Mountain Arts, Inc. All rights reserved. Reprinted with permission of Blue Mountain Arts, Inc.

Chapter 3

1. Ann Getzoff and Carolyn McClenahan, *Step Kids: A Survival Guide For Teenagers in Stepfamilies* (New York: Walker & Company, 1984), p. 161.

2. Linda Albert and Elizabeth Einstein, *Dealing With Discipline, A Stepfamily Living Booklet* (Lincoln, NE: Stepfamily Association of America, Inc., 1983).

3. Jane Nelsen, Ed.D., *Positive Discipline* (Fair Oaks, CA: Sunrise Press, 1981).

4. Getzoff and McClenahan, *Step Kids: A Survival Guide for Teenagers in Stepfamilies*, p. 12.

5. Patricia Papernow, Ph.D, "A Baby in the House," *Stepfamily Bulletin* (Winter 1984; Stepfamily Association of America, Inc.).

6. Patricia Papernow, Ph.D. "Stepfamily Cycle — Seven Steps to Familydom," *Stepfamily Bulletin* (Fall 1986 and Winter 1987; Stepfamily Association of America, Inc.).

7. Mary MacCracken, *Turnabout Children* (Boston: Little, Brown and Co., Inc., 1986), p. 252.

Chapter 4

1. Barry Kaufman, *To Love Is to Be Happy With* (New York: Fawcett Crest Books, 1977), p. 234.

2. Rev. Neal Kuyper, "When Eight Is Enough," *Remarriage Newsletter* (Vol. 2, No. 9; September 1985).

3. Anthony Padovano, *Love and Destiny: Marriage as God's Gift* (Mahwah, NJ: Paulist Press, 1987), p. 54.

Chapter 5

1. C. S. Lewis, *The Four Loves* (New York: Harcourt, Brace, 1960).

2. "The true test of love reposes in tranquility," by syndicated columnist Sidney J. Harris (deceased) who wrote for the *Chicago Daily News* and the *Chicago Sun Times*.

3. C. William Tageson, "Why Love Is So Complicated," *Notre Dame Magazine* (Spring 1984, Vol. 13, No. 2).

4. Susan Polis Schutz, "I often wonder what. . ." Copyright © 1984, Stephen Schutz and Susan Polis Schutz. All rights reserved. Reprinted by permission of Continental Publications.

5. Kahlil Gibran, "On Marriage" from *The Prophet* (New York: Alfred A. Knopf, Publisher, 1985), pp. 15–16.

6. Excerpted with permission from Ardis Whitman, "The Invitation to Live" (*Reader's Digest*, April 1972. Copyright © 1972 by The Reader's Digest Association, Inc.).

7. M. Scott Peck, M.D., *The Road Less Traveled* (New York: Touchstone Books, Simon and Schuster, 1978).

8. Sidney Simon, *Caring, Feeling, Touching* (Niles, IL: Argus Communications, 1976), pp. 8–9.

9. John Powell, *The Secret of Staying in Love*. Copyright © 1974, Tabor Publishing, a division of DLM, Inc., Allen, TX 75002.

Chapter 6

1. Richard J. Sweeney, "How God Invites Us to Grow," *Catholic Update* (CU1087, October 1987; St. Anthony Messenger Press).

2. Harold S. Kushner, *When Bad Things Happen to Good People*, Copyright © 1987, Avon Publishing Company, p. 146.

3. Mary and James Kenny, "The Sacrament of Marriage," *Catholic Update* (CU0979, 1979; St. Anthony Messenger Press).

4. Virginia Smith, "The Four Faces of Jesus," *Catholic Update* (CU 0390, March 1990; St. Anthony Messenger Press).

5. Jeffrey Keefe, O.F.M. Conv., "Why the Church Is Granting More Annulments," *Catholic Update* (CU 1080, 1980; St. Anthony Messenger Press).

6. *Annulment: Do You Have a Case?*, Rev. Terence E. Tierney, J.C.L.; Alba House, New York, 1978. Other resources on annulments include: Joseph P. Zwack, *Annulment — Your Chance to Remarry Within the Catholic Church* (San Francisco: Harper & Row, 1983) and James J. Young, CSP, editor, *Divorce Ministry and the Marriage Tribunal* (Mahwah, NJ: Paulist Press, 1982).

7. Ann Weems, *Reaching for Rainbows*, Copyright © 1980 The Westminster Press. Reprinted and used by permission of Westminster/John Knox Press.

Resources

Stepfamily Association of America, Inc.
215 S. Centennial Mall, Ste. 212
Lincoln, NE 68508
(402) 477–7837

The North American Conference of Separated and Divorced
  Catholics, Inc.
1100 Goodman Street
Rochester, NY 14620
(716) 271–1320

New Beginnings: Divorce Recovery
Once More With Love
6098 Guadalupe Mines Road
San Jose, CA 95120

Bibliography

General

Make Your Tomorrow Better, Michael E. Cavanagh, Ph.D.; Paulist Press, 1980.

Rebuilding: When Your Relationship Ends, Bruce Fisher; Impact Publishers, 1981.

Surviving the Breakup, Judith Wallerstein and Joan Kelly; Basic Books, Inc., 1980.

The Road Less Traveled, M. Scott Peck, M.D.; Simon and Schuster, 1978.

The Secret of Staying in Love, John Powell, S.J.; Tabor Publishing, 1974.

When Bad Things Happen to Good People, Harold S. Kushner; Avon Books, 1981.

Communication

Caring Enough to Confront, David Augsburger; Herald Press, 1981.

Discovering the Enneagram — An Ancient Tool for a New Spiritual Journey, Richard Rohr and Andreas Ebert; Crossroad Publishing Company, 1990.

Do I Have to Give Up Me to Be Loved By You? Jordan and Margaret Paul; CompCare Publications, 1983.

Getting Together — Building Relationships as We Negotiate, Roger Fisher and Scott Brown; Penguin Books, 1988.

Please Understand Me — Character & Temperament Types, David Keirsey and Marilyn Bates; Prometheus Nemesis Books, 1978.

The Enneagram — A Journey of Self Discovery, Maria Beesing, O.P., Robert J. Nogosek, C.S.C., and Patrick H. O'Leary, S.J.; Dimension Books, Inc., 1984.

Stepfamilies

All About Families the Second Time Around, Helen Coale Lewis; Peachtree Publishers Ltd., 1980 (Adults and Children).

How to Discipline Children Without Feeling Guilty, Harris Clemes and Reynold Bean; Enrich, 1980.

How to Teach Your Child Right From Wrong, Sr. Joel Campbell, O.P. and Sr. Patricia Knopp, S.N.D.; Claretian Publications, 1977.

Mom's House, Dad's House: Making Shared Custody Work, Isolina Ricci, Ph.D; Collier Books, Macmillan Publishers, 1980.

Now I Have a Stepparent, Janet Sinbergstenson; Avon Publishers, 1979 (Children).

101 Ways to Be a Long Distance Super-Dad, George Newman; Stepfamily Association.

Parent Effectiveness Training (P.E.T.), Dr. Thomas Gordon; New American Library, 1975.

Positive Discipline, Jane Nelsen, Ed.D.; Sunrise Press, 1981.

Stepfamilies — Myths and Realities, John and Emily Visher; Citadel Press, 1979.

Stepkids — A Survival Guide for Teenagers in Stepfamilies, Ann Getzoff and Carolyn McClenahan; Walker and Company, 1984.

Strengthening Your Stepfamily, Elizabeth Einstein and Linda Albert; American Guidance Service, 1986.

What Am I Doing in a Stepfamily?, Claire G. Berman; Lyle Stuart Inc., 1982 (Children).

Your Child's Self-Esteem, Dorothy Corkille Briggs; Doubleday Dolphin Books, 1975.

Finances

Premarital Agreements — When, Why, and How to Write Them, Joseph P. Zwack; Harper and Row, 1987.

Intimacy

Love Is Letting Go of Fear, Gerald G. Jampolsky, M.D.; Bantam Books, 1970.

Sex, If I Didn't Laugh, I'd Cry, Jess Lair; Doubleday, 1979.

The Art of Learning to Love Yourself, Cecil G. Osborne; Zondervan Publishers, 1979.

The Couple's Journey, Susan M. Campbell; Impact Publishers, 1980.

Why Am I Afraid to Tell You Who I Am?, John Powell; Argus Communications, 1969.

Religion

Annulment: Do You Have a Case?, Rev. Terence E. Tierney, J.C.L.; Alba House, 1978.

Annulment: Your Chance to Remarry Within the Catholic Church, Joseph P. Zwack; Harper and Row, 1983.

Divorce and Second Marriage, Kevin T. Kelly; Seabury Press, 1983.

Divorce Ministry and the Marriage Tribunal, James J. Young, C.S.P., Editor; Paulist Press, 1982.

Divorcing, Believing, Belonging, James J. Young, C.S.P.; Paulist Press, 1984.

Healing the Wounds of Divorce, Barbara Leahy Shlemon, Ave Maria Press, 1992.

Marriage: Sacrament of Hope and Challenge, Will P. Roberts; St. Anthony Messenger Press, 1988.

New Hope for Divorced Catholics, Fr. Barry Brunsman; Harper & Row, 1985.

To Know and Follow Jesus, Thomas N. Hart; Paulist Press, 1984.

When Catholics Marry Again, Gerald S. Twomey; Winston Press, 1982.

Facilitator's Guide

For those planning group use of *Once More With Love* as a remarriage preparation program, a handy Facilitator's Guide is available *directly from the author.*

This Guide includes:
   ◆ Instructions on how to use *Once More With Love* as a remarriage preparation program

   ◆ Six lesson plans

   ◆ Bibliography

   ◆ Sample publicity

Please make checks payable to:
New Beginnings: Divorce Recovery

Mail order with payment directly to:
New Beginnings: Divorce Recovery
6098 Guadalupe Mines Road
San Jose, CA 95120

Please send _____copies of *Once More With Love* Facilitator's Guide @ $8.00 each. (Include $2.50 for one, and $.50 for each additional copy, to cover postage and handling.)

Name _____

Address _____

City _____ State _____ Zip code _____